OXFORD WOR~~LD'S CLASSICS~~

A CASE

T0083412

SIGMUND FREUD was born in ~~Moravia~~, but was brought to
Vienna by his parents at the age of 4 and lived there until his flight
to England after the German annexation of Austria in 1938. Having
received a broad classical education, he trained as a doctor at the
Vienna Medical School. He worked initially on the nervous system,
then became interested in the therapeutic uses of cocaine, in speech
disorders, and in using hypnosis in treating psychological afflictions.
His *Studies in Hysteria* (1895), written jointly with his older colleague
Josef Breuer, maintained that 'hysterics suffer mainly from reminis-
cences' which could be recalled and discharged by the 'talking cure'.
In 1897, however, Freud concluded that hysterical and neurotic
patients most often suffered from fantasies stemming from their relations with their parents in childhood. He embarked on the investigation of unconscious fantasy–life which produced *The Interpretation
of Dreams* (1899), *The Psychopathology of Everyday Life* (1901), and
Jokes and their Relation to the Unconscious (1905). His *Three Essays on
the Theory of Sexuality* (1905) argued that patterns of sexual development, involving such mechanisms as identification and repression,
were central to the unconscious forces shaping the personality. From
there he developed psychoanalysis as a therapeutic technique and a
theory of the unconscious which underwent many mutations, both in
Freud's work and in that of followers, from Jung onwards, who suc-
cessively established independent schools of psychoanalytic thought
and treatment. Freud died in exile in Hampstead in 1939.

ANTHEA BELL is a freelance translator from French and German, and
the winner of many translation awards. She has translated the
entire *Asterix* series, with Derek Hockridge, and many adult novels,
including W. G. Sebald's *Austerlitz*, a large selection of novellas
and stories by Stefan Zweig, and E. T. A. Hoffmann's *The Life and
Opinions of the Tomcat Murr*. She has translated Kafka's *The Castle* for
Oxford World's Classics.

RITCHIE ROBERTSON is Taylor Professor of German at Oxford and
a Fellow of the Queen's College. He is the author of *Kafka: A Very
Short Introduction* and the translator of *The Man who Disappeared* for
Oxford World's Classics, in which series he has also provided the
introductions and notes for four other Kafka translations. He is the
editor of *The Cambridge Companion to Thomas Mann* and the author
of *Mock-Epic Poetry from Pope to Heine*.

OXFORD WORLD'S CLASSICS

*For over 100 years Oxford World's Classics have brought
readers closer to the world's great literature. Now with over 700
titles—from the 4,000-year-old myths of Mesopotamia to the
twentieth century's greatest novels—the series makes available
lesser-known as well as celebrated writing.*

*The pocket-sized hardbacks of the early years contained
introductions by Virginia Woolf, T. S. Eliot, Graham Greene,
and other literary figures which enriched the experience of reading.
Today the series is recognized for its fine scholarship and
reliability in texts that span world literature, drama and poetry,
religion, philosophy, and politics. Each edition includes perceptive
commentary and essential background information to meet the
changing needs of readers.*

OXFORD WORLD'S CLASSICS

═══

SIGMUND FREUD

A Case of Hysteria
(Dora)

═══

Translated by
ANTHEA BELL

With an Introduction and Notes by
RITCHIE ROBERTSON

OXFORD
UNIVERSITY PRESS

OXFORD
UNIVERSITY PRESS

Great Clarendon Street, Oxford OX2 6DP
United Kingdom

Oxford University Press is a department of the University of Oxford.
It furthers the University's objective of excellence in research, scholarship,
and education by publishing worldwide. Oxford is a registered trade mark of
Oxford University Press in the UK and in certain other countries

Translation © Anthea Bell 2013
Editorial material © Ritchie Robertson 2013

The moral rights of the authors have been asserted

First published as an Oxford World's Classics paperback 2013

Impression: 11

British Library Cataloguing in Publication Data
Data available

ISBN 978–0–19–963986–1

Printed in Great Britain by
Clays Ltd, Elcograf S.p.A.

CONTENTS

INTRODUCTION

FREUD'S 'Fragment of an Analysis of a Case of Hysteria', popularly known, after the patient's pseudonym, as the case of 'Dora', is one of the very few case histories that he wrote, and therefore a rare piece of evidence about how he actually formed his interpretations in sessions of analysis. Strictly speaking there are only three case histories. The others are the stories of the 'Rat Man', a Viennese Jewish lawyer called Ernst Lanzer who suffered from the fear that rats would enter and devour his anus, and the 'Wolf Man', a Russian aristocrat called Sergey Pankeyev whose severe depression Freud traced back to a childhood dream of six or seven white wolves staring at him from a tree outside his bedroom window.[1] The essay on 'Little Hans' hardly counts as a case history, since Freud met the five-year-old Herbert Graf only once and relied mainly on reports from his father Max Graf; while Freud's study of the insane judge Daniel Paul Schreber was based entirely on a reading of Schreber's extraordinary memoirs.[2]

So the three case histories, few in number and bizarre in content, form the empirical material which generations of psychoanalysts have studied as part of their training. They were described in 1965 by the émigré analyst Kurt Eissler as 'the pillars on which psychoanalysis as an empirical science rests'.[3] A close study of Freud's account of 'Dora', therefore, will reveal much about what Freud did with the material presented to him and about

---

[1] See 'Notes upon a Case of Obsessional Neurosis', *The Standard Edition of the Complete Psychological Works of Sigmund Freud*, ed. James Strachey, 24 vols. (London: Hogarth Press, 1953–74) [henceforth SE], x. 155–249; 'From the History of an Infantile Neurosis', SE xvii. 7–122; Patrick J. Mahony, *Freud and the Rat Man* (New Haven and London: Yale University Press, 1986); Karin Obholzer, *The Wolf-Man Sixty Years After* (London: Routledge & Kegan Paul, 1982).

[2] 'Analysis of the Phobia in a Five-Year-Old Boy', SE x. 5–149); 'Psycho-Analytic Notes on an Autobiographical Account of a Case of Paranoia (Dementia Paranoides)', SE xii. 9–82.

[3] Quoted in Mikkel Borch-Jacobsen and Sonu Shamdasani, *The Freud Files: An Inquiry into the History of Psychoanalysis* (Cambridge: Cambridge University Press, 2012), 184.

the basis on which psychoanalysis can claim to be an empirical science, or, more modestly, a source of knowledge about the human mind and of therapy for emotional disorders. It will also provide a fuller view than any other text of what went on in Freud's consulting-room.

The Facts in the Case of 'Dora'

It is not easy to separate the empirical material in the case history from Freud's interpretations. Much that is presented as fact turns out, on closer scrutiny, to be a second-hand account or a conjecture, whether by Freud or by his patient. The following account is intended as minimalist.

The ascertainable facts about 'Dora' and her family are these. Her real name was Ida Bauer.[4] She was born on 1 November 1882 at Berggasse 32—the same Viennese street where Freud lived—to a well-to-do middle-class Jewish family. Her only sibling, Otto, born on 5 September 1881, would become a leading Marxist theorist, parliamentary secretary to the Austrian Social Democratic Party, and a prominent politician in the First Austrian Republic. Their father, Philipp Bauer, born in Bohemia on 14 August 1853, was a successful textile manufacturer, with factories in two northern Bohemian towns, Warnsdorf (now Varnsdorf) and Nachod (now Náchod, both in the Czech Republic). At the age of twenty-seven, after a two-year engagement, he had married the eighteen-year-old Katharina Gerber (born in 1862). They lived initially in the Leopoldstadt district of Vienna, known as the poorer Jewish quarter, then traded up to Berggasse in the more prosperous Ninth District.

Although a highly energetic businessman, Philipp had poor physical health. He had been virtually blind in one eye since birth.

---

[4] On her identity, see the long footnote in Peter Loewenberg, 'Austro-Marxism and Revolution: Otto Bauer, Freud's "Dora" Case, and the Crises of the First Austrian Republic', in his *Decoding the Past: The Psychohistorical Approach* (New York: Knopf, 1983), 161–204 (pp. 162–3), based on both written and oral sources. Hannah S. Decker has confirmed this information by consulting the records of the Israelitische Kultusgemeinde Wien: see her *Freud, Dora, and Vienna 1900* (New York: Free Press, 1991).

In 1888 he was diagnosed with tuberculosis. He handed over the active management of his business to his elder brother Karl (1848–1916), described by Freud as 'a bachelor and a hypochondriac' (p. 15), and moved with his family to the Alpine health resort of Meran (now Merano in Italy) in what was then the Austrian province of South Tyrol. In 1892 he developed a detached retina in his good eye and was temporarily blind until, by what seemed a miracle, his previously unusable eye developed enough sight for him to read and write.

The worst, however, was yet to come. In 1894 he suffered mental disturbance and partial paralysis. On the advice of Hans Zellenka, a shopkeeper he had got to know in Meran, Philipp consulted Freud, who already had a high reputation as a neurologist. The symptoms were the manifestation of syphilis which Philipp had contracted before his marriage and which was now entering its tertiary stage. Freud prescribed an anti-syphilitic treatment, after which the symptoms vanished. Philipp had, however, infected his wife, if not with syphilis (as their daughter apparently believed), then with gonorrhoea, which in women causes severe abdominal pains.[5] Both mother and daughter suffered also from a vaginal discharge which Freud calls *fluor albus* and which they called catarrh; they sometimes stayed in the Bohemian health resort of Franzensbad (Františkovy Lázně) in the hope of alleviation. Venereal disease was then, and for long afterwards, supposed to be hereditary as well as infectious, and Ida apparently believed she had inherited syphilis from her father.

Katharina Bauer presumably had no idea that her husband was syphilitic when she married him. Ida gave Freud reason to think that she found out when a doctor suggested a venereal origin for the detached retina. After this, Katharina withdrew emotionally from her husband. Various witnesses attest that she was preoccupied to the point of obsession with cleaning the family apartment. The public rooms were kept locked to avoid dirt, and the whole flat received a specially thorough cleaning every Friday, when the family had to keep out of it.[6]

---

[5] See Decker, *Freud, Dora, and Vienna*, 51.

[6] See ibid. 54.

Ida herself had a history of ill-health starting in 1890, when she was seven, with an attack of dyspnoea or difficulty in breathing. Four years later she fell ill with migraine, aphonia (inability to speak aloud), and a chronic cough. She was treated with electrotherapy and hydrotherapy. The former probably consisted in having an electrical current applied to various parts of her body, beginning with the forehead, the temples, the top and back of the head, the neck, and so down the spinal column, two to four times a week. Hydrotherapy meant receiving a jet of cold water for fifteen seconds at a time, in order to produce a salutary shock.[7] These treatments had no effect. In 1898 her father took her to see Freud, who recommended psychological treatment, but as Ida's hoarseness and coughing got better spontaneously, this advice was not followed. Ida appears not to have attended school but to have been taught at home by a governess and sometimes to have attended public lectures.[8] She spent a lot of time taking care of her father. We must imagine her teenage years as completely overshadowed by illness—her own and that of other people.

Ida's return to Freud in October 1900, which gave rise to the famous case history, was prompted by something else. Not only Hans Zellenka, who had advised Philipp to consult Freud in the first place, but also his wife Peppina (Giuseppina Heumann, born on 20 March 1870), were friendly with the Bauer family, and Peppina helped to nurse Philipp.[9] Ida told Freud that this had led to a love-affair between Philipp and Peppina. For a time, Ida seemed not to object, indeed she and Peppina were close friends, and Ida looked after the Zellenkas' two children, Otto (born 5 January 1891) and Clara (born 26 December 1891); the latter suffered from a congenital heart defect. After consulting Freud in summer 1898, Ida and her father went on to visit the Zellenkas, who were spending the summer at an Alpine lakeside resort.

[7] See Decker, *Freud, Dora, and Vienna*, 9–12.

[8] Decker's surmise (ibid. 57) that she attended the local convent school is corrected on the basis of further inquiries by Patrick J. Mahony, *Freud's Dora: A Psychoanalytic, Historical, and Textual Study* (New Haven and London: Yale University Press, 1996), 6.

[9] Data about the Zellenkas and their children come from Mahony, *Freud's Dora*, 7. Mahony's 'Guiseppina' is probably a typographical error.

Although the plan had been for Ida to stay longer with the Zellenkas after her father's departure, she insisted on returning with him. A few days later, she told her mother, who told her father, who later told Freud, that Herr Zellenka, while walking with her beside the lake, had made a sexual proposition to her, whereupon she slapped his face and ran away. Called to account by Herr Bauer and his brother, Herr Zellenka flatly denied it. Thereafter, Ida repeatedly urged her father to break off relations with the Zellenkas, which he refused to do. Over the next two years—during which the Bauers left Meran, moved briefly to Reichenberg (Liberec) near Philipp's factories in Bohemia, and then returned to the Ninth District of Vienna—she got on very badly with both her parents. The Zellenkas first stayed behind in Meran, then moved to Vienna very shortly after the Bauers had moved there. Ida alarmed her parents by writing them a note saying she intended to kill herself because her life was unbearable. Soon afterwards, while arguing with her father, she fainted, and, on recovering, had no memory of the incident. This, and Ida's continuing antipathy to the Zellenkas, determined her father, despite her reluctance, to bring her back to Freud, which he did with the words: 'Please try to bring her round to a better way of thinking' (p. 21).

These are the facts that are known with reasonable certainty. Everything else in the case is report, conjecture, interpretation.

A Bourgeois Jewish Family

Before we enter into Freud's treatment of the case, it is worth reflecting on Steven Marcus's description of it as 'a classical Victorian domestic drama, that is at the same time a sexual and emotional can of worms'.[10] The Bauer family may have been unhappy in a remarkably horrible way, but in their misery the

---

[10] Steven Marcus, 'Freud and Dora: Story, History, Case History', in his *Representations: Essays on Literature and Society* (New York: Random House, 1976), 247–310 (p. 253). This important essay is also available in Charles Bernheimer and Claire Kahane (eds.), *In Dora's Case: Freud—Hysteria—Feminism* (New York: Columbia University Press, 1985).

Bauers were to a large extent living out possibilities that were always present in the bourgeois family.[11]

While the dominant role of the father comes as no surprise, we might also note the ready cooperation among men. Philipp Bauer brings his daughter to Freud and urges the latter to deal with her. Ida suspected—as we shall soon see—an unpleasant collusion between her father and Herr Zellenka over the former's relationship with the latter's wife. We shall also see that Freud, analysing the case, unwittingly identifies with Philipp Bauer and still more with Hans Zellenka. Katharina Bauer, meanwhile, receives no sympathy from anyone. Freud dismisses her as an uneducated and foolish woman who fell victim to a 'housewife psychosis' (p. 15). But one might have more sympathy with a person confined to the monotonous drudgery of housework.[12] In subjecting the family to her domestic tyranny, she was surely, as Decker points out, trying to 'retain some fragments of power' in a life where she lacked control even over her own body.[13] She locked the dining-room at night, which meant locking Otto in his bedroom, as it could only be reached via the dining-room; and she alone had the key to the sideboard where her husband's brandy was kept. Confined to a domestic role, she took house-cleaning to obsessive lengths, perhaps as a form of revenge. 'You have made me a housewife; very well, I'll be a perfect housewife and make you suffer for it.'

In this milieu, education was highly valued, but only for boys. Otto Bauer attended a classical *Gymnasium* in Meran, where he acquired a thorough education in the Greek and Latin classics, along with German, history, geography, mathematics, physics, and French and English. If the Bauers had lived in Vienna, Ida might have attended a *Mädchen-Lyzeum*, where a relatively undemanding curriculum, with modern instead of classical languages, was available: in 1910/11, 45.4 per cent of pupils in Viennese

[11] On this subject I am indebted to Peter Gay, *The Bourgeois Experience: Victoria to Freud*, 5 vols. (New York: Oxford University Press, 1984–98). Gay deals with the inevitable difficulties of defining 'bourgeois' in vol. 1, *Education of the Senses* (1984), 17–44.

[12] See the extracts from the diary of an anonymous nineteenth-century Connecticut housewife, quoted in Gay, *Bourgeois Experience*, i. 172–3.

[13] Decker, *Freud, Dora, and Vienna*, 55.

girls' secondary schools were Jewish.[14] If she was educated by her
governess, however, her appetite for learning, which Freud mentions with no sign of interest, probably received little satisfaction.
She may have envied her brother his access to education; this,
however, like her relationship to her brother generally, finds no
mention in Freud's text.[15] Freud himself shared the conventional
view that women belonged in the home. Writing to his fiancée in
1883, he deplored the unrealistic programme for the equality of
the sexes put forward by John Stuart Mill in *The Subjection of
Women*, which he had himself translated into German.[16]

Austria had its feminist movement, but the General Austrian
Women's Association, established in 1893 with the determined
feminist Auguste Fickert as its secretary, had far fewer members
than its antagonist, the anti–Semitic and anti-emancipatory
Viennese Christian Women's League, founded in the same year.[17]
Even such a devastating cultural critic as Karl Kraus, who cam-
paigned against the illiberal and hypocritical laws on prostitution, did not support female emancipation through education,
as it would weaken the intrinsically erotic character which
distinguished woman from the predominantly intellectual man.[18]
However, women were admitted to Vienna University, though
initially only to the arts faculty, from 1897 onwards. The prominent Viennese feminist Rosa Mayreder argued that women's education should equip them for motherhood, but that they should
not see their destiny as confined to the roles of wife and mother:

The woman who omits to develop any special talent of her own
because of her belief that it is possible to 'develop' it in her son, will, in

[14] Decker, ibid. 57; Marsha L. Rozenblit, *The Jews of Vienna: Assimilation and Identity*
(Albany, NY: State University of New York Press, 1983), 121.

[15] This absence is noted by Juliet Mitchell, *Mad Men and Medusas: Reclaiming
Hysteria* (New York: Basic Books, 2000), pp. 100–7.

[16] *Letters of Sigmund Freud*, ed. Ernst L. Freud, tr. Tania and James Stern (London:
The Hogarth Press, 1961), 90–1. See Estelle Roith, *The Riddle of Freud: Jewish Influences
on his Theory of Female Sexuality* (London and New York: Tavistock Publications, 1987),
120–1.

[17] Harriet Anderson, *Utopian Feminism: Women's Movements in fin-de-siècle Vienna*
(New Haven and London: Yale University Press, 1992), 42.

[18] See Edward Timms, *Karl Kraus, Apocalyptic Satirist: Culture and Crisis in Habsburg
Vienna* (New Haven and London: Yale University Press, 1986), 63–93.

ninety-nine cases out of a hundred, be grievously cheated of the fruits of her life. Why not live your own lives, dear mothers, and thereby spare your children all these immense burdens of hopes and wishes which they must bear with them under the supposition that their duty in life is to please you and not themselves![19]

Wives and daughters were not the only female members of the bourgeois household. There were servants, including nursemaids, and the Bauers had a governess for Ida. Domestic servants were ready targets for philandering employers, and a solitary governess was particularly exposed (think of *Jane Eyre*). In 1904 a statistical study of illegitimate births in German and Austrian cities found that in Vienna and Berlin over a third of all illegitimate children were born to domestic servants.[20] We shall presently see that governesses played a significant role in Ida's recollections. A governess could also provide her charge with knowledge of the world, including sexual knowledge, which a well-brought-up girl was not supposed to have. She could provide a boy with early sexual experience: another of Freud's famous patients, the 'Rat Man', at the age of six, was allowed by his governess to feel her genitals.[21] Thus the bourgeois family, supposedly secure against the outside world, was in fact highly permeable: 'Sexuality leaks, and sometimes bursts, into the family cell through the channel of the nurse, the governess, the maid.'[22]

Relations between the sexes were threatened by venereal disease. Sexually active young men, who were expected to marry relatively late, like Philipp Bauer, readily resorted to prostitutes.

[19] Rosa Mayreder, *A Survey of the Woman Problem*, tr. Herman Scheffauer (London: Heinemann, 1913), 67–8. Originally published as *Zur Kritik der Weiblichkeit* (1905).

[20] Gay, *The Bourgeois Experience*, vol. 2: *The Tender Passion* (1986), 408–9.

[21] Freud, SE x. 160. In 1896 Freud claimed that sexual relations with children were often initiated by a variety of adults—governesses, nursery-maids, tutors, or close relatives—or by other children (SE iii. 163–5, 207), and in a letter of 4 October 1897 he told his close friend Wilhelm Fliess that his own nurse was 'my teacher in sexual matters and complained because I was clumsy and unable to do anything': *The Complete Letters of Sigmund Freud to Wilhelm Fliess, 1887–1904*, tr. and ed. J. M. Masson (Cambridge, Mass., and London: Belknap Press, 1985), 269. It is not clear whether this was an actual memory or Freud's inference from one of his own dreams.

[22] Lisa Appignanesi and John Forrester, *Freud's Women* (London: Weidenfeld & Nicolson, 1992), 162.

Introduction   xv

Prostitution was often claimed to be essential to satisfy male libido
and thus to safeguard the purity of the bourgeois household.[23]
The case of the Bauer family indicates, on the contrary, that prostitution made the family vulnerable to infection. Men, once
infected, might well persist in vice. Arthur Schnitzler tells a
revealing story about an incautious friend of his, Richard
Tausenau, who picked up an infection, but did not change his
ways. Shortly afterwards the two men drew lots for a chorus-girl,
but Schnitzler, a medical student, felt a suspicious gland on her
neck and resigned her to his friend, who could afford to take the
risk.[24] Venereal disease was thought to be widespread: the British
suffragette Christabel Pankhurst declared that at least three-
quarters of Victorian men were infected with gonorrhoea, and 'a
considerable percentage' with syphilis (though one should allow
for the tendency of reformers to base their cases on wild guess-
work and possibly also on self-serving exaggeration).[25] It was also
generally believed that syphilis was hereditary and that syphilitic
men would father deformed, disabled, hideous, and short-lived
children. Doctors and moralists issued dire warnings, but the
methods that might have done something to check the spread of
syphilis—publicity and contraception—were severely discour-
aged. Boys were warned against syphilis, but girls were supposed
to know nothing about it. Young men took risks, often in the spirit
of a dare, and if after marriage they infected their wives, the
scandal was hushed up.[26] Some notorious plays—Ibsen's *Ghosts*,
Eugène Brieux's *Les Avariés* (*The Diseased*, 1901), and in Austria,
Ludwig Anzengruber's *Das vierte Gebot* (*The Fourth Commandment*,
1877)—dramatized the issue of hereditary disease.[27] Freud's case
history may have helped further to break the taboo on the subject.

[23] Gay, *Bourgeois Experience*, ii. 363.
[24] Arthur Schnitzler, *Jugend in Wien*, ed. Therese Nickl and Heinrich Schnitzler
(Vienna: Molden, 1968), 176.
[25] Pankhurst, *The Great Scourge and How To End It* (1913), quoted in Elaine Showalter,
Sexual Anarchy: Gender and Culture at the Fin de Siècle (London: Virago, 1992), 197.
[26] A well-known case is the Danish writer 'Isak Dinesen' (Karen Blixen), who was
infected with syphilis by her promiscuous husband in 1914: see Judith Thurman, *Isak
Dinesen: The Life of Karen Blixen* (1982; Harmondsworth: Penguin, 1984), 149–54.
[27] On the scandalized reception of *Ghosts* in Scandinavia, see Michael Meyer, *Ibsen*
(Stroud: Sutton, 2004), 348–52; in London, Showalter, *Sexual Anarchy*, 200, and the

Many bourgeois families were plagued by less lurid but still often disabling illnesses. In the later nineteenth century it was generally believed that the increased pace of modern urban life harmed people's nerves and caused such afflictions as nervous exhaustion (called 'neurasthenia'), hypochondria, and hysteria.[28] Freud argued in 1908 that modern nervousness, far from having an undiscovered organic cause as many physicians assumed, resulted from the sexual repression and self-control required by bourgeois civilization.[29] Family pressures can also be blamed. There are famous examples of women confined for long periods to sick-rooms with ailments which seem at least in part to have been psychosomatic. Ida Bauer can be added to a long list of female invalids which includes Elizabeth Barrett Browning, Florence Nightingale, and Alice James (sister of the philosopher William James and the novelist Henry James).[30] Thus Eliza Wilson, the future wife of Walter Bagehot, resembled her mother in suffering from migraines and eye-strain; Peter Gay observes that Bagehot too 'had intermittent crippling headaches and accepted her psychosomatic symptoms, like his own, as most nineteenth-century bourgeois accepted them: with resignation, practically as a matter of course'.[31] Psychosomatic illness could be a way of internalizing the oppressive restrictions of the bourgeois household, but also a means of manipulating the rest of the household: Ida's illnesses suggest both.

---

anthology of press quotations in Bernard Shaw, *The Quintessence of Ibsenism*, in his *Major Critical Essays* (London: Constable, 1932), 70–1. On Brieux's *Les Avariés*, see Claude Quétel, *History of Syphilis*, tr. Judith Braddock and Brian Pike (Cambridge: Polity, 1990), 152–8. Anzengruber's play is named after the commandment 'Honour thy father and thy mother' (Deuteronomy 5: 16), which is counted as the fourth of the Ten Commandments in the Catholic and Lutheran churches, but as the fifth in the Church of England. In it, a young woman, too obedient to her parents, marries a debauchee and has a short-lived child; the hint of syphilis is more discreet than in Ibsen.

[28] See Gay, *Bourgeois Experience*, ii. 330–52.

[29] Freud, '"Civilized" Sexual Morality and Modern Nervousness', SE ix. 181–204. Cf. Gay, *Bourgeois Experience*, ii. 349–52.

[30] See Daniel Karlin, *The Courtship of Robert Browning and Elizabeth Barrett* (Oxford: Clarendon Press, 1985); Jean Strouse, *Alice James: A Biography* (1980; New York: New York Review Books, 2011), esp. 97–131; Brian Dillon, *Tormented Hope: Nine Hypochondriac Lives* (2009; London: Penguin, 2010), esp. 107–11 on Nightingale's unidentifiable illness and 112–13 for her complaint about women's enforced idleness.

[31] Gay, *Bourgeois Experience*, ii. 20; cf. ii. 119.

The Bauers, like the Freuds, belonged specifically to the Jewish middle class.[32] Hannah Decker has argued that they lived in an insecurity that helped predispose Ida to hysteria, and the claim deserves consideration. Vienna had a large Jewish population, almost 9 per cent in 1900, but more than half of this population was concentrated in three districts—the First, Second, and Ninth—and, within those districts, in particular streets and apartment blocks. Hence, when one explores the references to people in Freud's works and personal writings, one has the sense of a quite close-knit community where everybody is a relation or colleague of everybody else.[33] However, Viennese Jews, especially as they rose in the social scale and absorbed Western culture, became detached from Jewish tradition and religious practice. They celebrated Christmas like their fellow-citizens: Ida Bauer mentions a Christmas present; Theodor Herzl, who published *The Jewish State* in 1896, was embarrassed the year before when the Chief Rabbi of Vienna called on him just as he was decorating a Christmas tree for his children.[34] Their Jewish identity had less and less Jewish content. In his treatise on nationalism, Otto Bauer described the Jews as a people without a history, whose culture belonged to the remote past, and who should be absorbed into the surrounding population instead of receiving the national autonomy which he proposed for other groups.[35]

[32] Sander Gilman has based an elaborate interpretation of Freud's text on the claim that Freud concealed Philipp Bauer's identity as an Eastern European Jew who, in the beliefs of the time, was hypersexual and especially prone to syphilis and hysteria: 'The Jewish Psyche: Freud, Dora, and the Idea of the Hysteric', in Gilman, *The Jew's Body* (New York and London: Routledge, 1995), 60–103. But a Jew from Bohemia did not necessarily fit the contemporary stereotype of the Eastern Jew or 'Ostjude'. See Steven E. Aschheim, *Brothers and Strangers: The East European Jew in German and German Jewish Consciousness, 1800–1923* (Madison, Wisc.: University of Wisconsin Press, 1982). Still less can 'Dora' be called 'the Eastern European Jew Ida Bauer': Gilman, *The Case of Sigmund Freud: Medicine and Identity at the Fin de Siècle* (Baltimore and London: Johns Hopkins University Press, 1993), 127.

[33] Cf. the testimony of Freud's son Martin, quoted in Decker, *Freud, Dora, and Vienna*, 31.

[34] Theodor Herzl, *Briefe und Tagebücher*, ed. Alex Bein *et al.*, 7 vols. (Berlin, Frankfurt a.M., and Vienna: Propyläen, 1983–96), ii. 288.

[35] See Loewenberg, 'Austro-Marxism and Revolution', 164–6; Otto Bauer, *Die Nationalitätenfrage und die Sozialdemokratie* (Vienna: Verlag der Wiener Volksbuchhandlung, 1924), 366–81.

Viennese Jews supported the liberal politics to which they owed their legal emancipation.[36] In *The Interpretation of Dreams*, Freud recalls wistfully the 'Bürgerministerium' or Bourgeois Ministry, the largely middle-class cabinet appointed by the emperor in 1868, which even included Jews, 'which meant that every industrious Jewish boy carried a ministerial portfolio in his satchel'.[37] After the liberal era ended with a change of ministry in 1879, Viennese Jews felt marginalized. Presently a new breed of populist politicians—first the Pan-German Georg von Schönerer, and later the Christian-Social Karl Lueger, who was mayor of Vienna from 1897 till his death in 1910—won support by using anti-Semitic rhetoric to denounce the Jewish press, businesses, and banks.[38] Lueger's rhetoric appealed to a poorly educated Catholic populace that was used to hearing Jews denounced as enemies of Christ. The year before Ida Bauer's analysis, the Bohemian village of Polna, not far from her father's factories, witnessed a charge of ritual murder against a Jewish man after a nineteen-year-old girl was found murdered; the Hilsner case was described at the time as 'the Austrian Dreyfus affair'.[39] Meanwhile, in 1897, the First Zionist Congress in Basel had publicized a new and, to most observers, impossibly hare-brained solution to what was called 'the Jewish question'. Against this background, there may well be a realistic justification for the view of the Viennese bourgeoisie that Schnitzler ascribes to the Gentile protagonist of his novel *Der Weg ins Freie* (*The Road to the Open*, 1908): 'Wherever he went, he met only Jews who were ashamed of being Jews, or others who were proud of it and afraid people might think they were ashamed.'[40]

[36] See Robert S. Wistrich, *The Jews of Vienna in the Age of Franz Joseph* (Oxford: Oxford University Press, 1989); Steven Beller, *Vienna and the Jews, 1867–1938: A Cultural History* (Cambridge: Cambridge University Press, 1989).

[37] Sigmund Freud, *The Interpretation of Dreams*, tr. Joyce Crick, Oxford World's Classics (Oxford: Oxford University Press, 1999), 148.

[38] See Carl E. Schorske, 'Politics in a New Key', in his *Fin-de-siècle Vienna: Politics and Culture* (Cambridge: Cambridge University Press, 1980), 116–80.

[39] František Červinka, 'The Hilsner Affair', *Leo Baeck Institute Year Book*, 13 (1968), 142–57 (p. 147); Decker, *Freud, Dora, and Vienna*, 83–4.

[40] Arthur Schnitzler, *Die Erzählenden Schriften*, 2 vols. (Frankfurt a.M.: Fischer, 1961), i. 661. My translation.

Among the contextual factors that encouraged Ida Bauer's hysteria, we may tentatively include the uneasy situation of Jews in Vienna, but also, more prominently, the tensions and conflicts within the tight-knit bourgeois family. It is no wonder that some searching critiques of the family came from the same Central European middle-class setting. Thus, the radical psychoanalyst Otto Gross combined Nietzschean individualism and Freud's conception of the unconscious to support his argument that the patriarchal family, which officially worshipped a patriarchal God conceived in the image of the father, stultified and stunted its members; he called for a revolution against the law of the father on behalf of the mother.[41] Franz Kafka, who met Gross at least twice and found him sympathetic, believed that children needed to be removed from the influence of both parents, who operated either through threats of violence or by much more insidious emotional blackmail, and entrusted to professional educators, who would respect the child and not regard it as their own possession.[42] These critiques owed a great deal, explicitly or implicitly, to Freud, for even if his own domestic and sexual attitudes were less than emancipatory, his inquiries into the emotional formation of his patients and the resulting theoretical constructions fatally weakened the authoritarian and hypocritical aspects of family life inherited from the nineteenth century.

Freud's Assumptions

Before we start examining Freud's text, we need to know what analytic equipment and assumptions he brought to the case. He was certain from the outset that Ida Bauer was hysterical. But it is not easy to say exactly what hysteria is or was. Ancient medical accounts do not use the word—it was added as a heading by Émile Littré to his nineteenth-century translation of the Hippocratic

[41] See Jennifer E. Michaels, *Anarchy and Eros: Otto Gross' Impact on German Expressionist Writers* (New York: Peter Lang, 1983).

[42] See Kafka's letters to his sister Elli Hermann, autumn 1921, in Kafka, *Briefe 1902–1924*, ed. Max Brod (Frankfurt a.M.: Fischer, 1958), 339–47; Kafka, *Letters to Friends, Family and Editors*, tr. Richard and Clara Winston (New York: Schocken, 1977), 290–7.

writings—but describe clusters of ailments in women such as difficulty in breathing, loss of voice, neck-pain, heart palpitations, dizziness, alongside symptoms such as blackening of the face that do not appear in more recent accounts, and ascribe them to the instability of the womb (Greek, *hystera*) in the female body. Subsequent explanations included demonic possession and sexual excess. The variety of explanations reflects the fact that hysteria is not a single, identifiable illness. It comprehends a wide range of transformations of emotional into physical suffering. The spectacular symptoms shown by nineteenth-century hysterics, such as convulsions and paralysis, are nowadays very rare. It may be that hysterical symptoms are now ascribed to bipolar disorder, borderline personality disorders, or anxiety neuroses; it may also be, as Elaine Showalter and Juliet Mitchell suggest, that recently prominent ways of registering suffering on the body, such as anorexia and bulimia, should be called hysterical. Nor need hysteria be thought of as typically female: the traumatic reactions to battlefield experience in the First World War, inadequately labelled 'shell-shock' at the time, and the post-traumatic stress disorder following recent conflicts can be seen as male hysteria. If hysteria is 'a universal human response to emotional conflict', common to women and men, it mimics the expressions of distress that are expected within a given culture.[43]

The great age of hysteria was the late nineteenth century. At a time when the increased pace of modern urban life was believed to damage the nervous system, a wide range of disorders were vaguely described as 'neurasthenia' or 'nervous suffering', with hysteria prominent among them. Religious and erotic theories were all dismissed by Jean-Martin Charcot, who explained hysteria as a dysfunction of the central nervous system which could also, though much more rarely, occur in men. At the Salpêtrière hospital in Paris, Charcot used to display the dramatic hysterical symptoms of his patients, amounting sometimes to convulsions, to medical students and curious visitors (including Freud).

[43] Elaine Showalter, *Hystories: Hysterical Epidemics and Modern Culture* (London: Picador, 1997), 15–20 (quotation from p. 17); Mitchell, *Mad Men and Medusas*, esp. 1–42.

Since Charcot, however, could not find an organic basis for hysteria, his professional rival Hippolyte Bernheim reconceptualized the condition in psychological terms, ascribing it to heightened suggestibility, while Pierre Janet transferred attention to the abnormal states of consciousness associated with hysteria and ascribed them to unresolved emotional traumas.

This is where Freud came in. A specialist in neuropathology, he was intrigued by his older colleague Josef Breuer's report on the patient Bertha Pappenheim, known as 'Anna O.'. In 1880, while nursing her father in his terminal illness, Bertha developed a florid array of symptoms, including paralysis in three limbs, a chronic cough, inability to eat, disturbances of vision, a dual personality, and hallucinations of black snakes. At one time she could not drink water, and had to live only on fruit. Hypnotized by Breuer, she complained of having seen a dog drink water out of a glass. She then asked for water, drank it, woke from hypnosis, and never suffered from this phobia again. Breuer induced her to talk about her other symptoms under hypnosis, and thus the 'talking cure' was born.

This standard account of 'Anna O.', however, can no longer pass unchallenged. A critical reading of the evidence suggests that Pappenheim was unhappy, suffocated by her family environment and by the strain of nursing her father; that she developed a 'hysterical' cough as a call for attention; that Breuer, summoned to cure her cough, undertook hypnosis and thus induced the further symptoms in response to his own expectations; and that the 'talking cure' did not cure Pappenheim, who gradually recovered her health only later in the decade and eventually found an active career in social work, the promotion of feminism, and combating the trafficking of Jewish women from Eastern Europe. Her original problem, in all likelihood, was not sexual frustration but simply frustration at being compelled to lead the subservient, restricted life that was imposed on so many young women in nineteenth-century bourgeois households.[44]

---

[44] See Appignanesi and Forrester, *Freud's Women*, 72–86; Mikkel Borch-Jacobsen, *Remembering Anna O.* (London: Routledge, 1996).

To learn more about the treatment of hysteria, Freud spent the winter of 1885–6 studying in Paris with Charcot. From the analyses he conducted back in Vienna, he concluded that hysteria resulted from the repression of traumatic memories with sexual content, and that hysterical symptoms could be interpreted as 'complex symbolizations of repressed psychological experiences'.[45] Symptoms were a language, and Freud was learning to read it. The message they disclosed was that the hysteric, frustrated in love, 'converted' her emotions into physical pains which we would nowadays call psychosomatic. Thus Ilona Weiss ('Fräulein Elisabeth von R.') 'succeeded in sparing herself the painful conviction that she loved her sister's husband, by inducing physical pains in herself instead' (SE ii. 157). The hidden message had to be sexual frustration.

When Ida Bauer was brought to him by her father in October 1900, therefore, Freud promptly identified her as a hysteric whose symptoms would be traceable to some unsatisfied sexual desire. At first the case seemed straightforward. On 14 October Freud told his Berlin correspondent Wilhelm Fliess that the case had 'smoothly opened to the existing collection of picklocks'.[46] Since he had treated the patients whose cases are described in the *Studies on Hysteria* (1895), however, Freud's collection had been enlarged in several important ways. One was the method of free association. The patient was encouraged to relax her concentration, let ideas float into her mind, and utter them, no matter how irrelevant they seemed. Ideas that emerged under these circumstances would not be random, but would reveal unconscious links which could be of the first importance in interpreting the patient's symptoms.

Free association was the basis of the method of dream-interpretation which Freud had been perfecting in the years before his treatment of Ida Bauer. He had published *The Interpretation of Dreams* in November 1899 (though the volume bore the date '1900'). His guiding assumption is that the dream represents the

[45] Mark S. Micale, *Approaching Hysteria: Disease and its Interpretations* (Princeton: Princeton University Press, 1995), 28.
[46] *Letters of Freud to Fliess*, 269.

fulfilment of a wish. However, the wish is usually something to which one does not consciously admit, and so the 'dream-work' hides it by a series of symbolic operations which the analyst must undo. Two different ideas may be run together ('condensation'); an emotional charge may be transferred from an important to a marginal element ('displacement'); the content must be adapted to the dream's representational resources, for example by eliminating causal and logical relations which cannot be represented in pictures, the dream's preferred medium; and finally, 'secondary revision' gives the dream a misleading semblance of coherence. Freud compares this method to the decipherment of ancient scripts or to solving a picture-puzzle such as a rebus. But these comparisons break down, because an ancient script cannot be deciphered unless one has some independent clue to its meaning, such as the Rosetta Stone, and because a rebus is decoded according to rules which are already known in outline. Neither of these applies to dream-interpretation.[47] The extreme flexibility which Freud attributes to the dream-work virtually obliges the interpreter to use a freedom that verges on the arbitrary.

In later editions of *The Interpretation of Dreams*, and under the influence of his follower Wilhelm Stekel, Freud tried to codify dream-interpretation by adopting the automatic translation of symbols into sexual meanings which has shaped the popular conception of Freudianism. Around 1900, however, he makes relatively little use of this technique. The main example to be found here is his automatic equation of the jewel-case in the first dream with the female genitals. At this period, however, Freud relies more heavily on word-play and on literary and cultural allusions. We shall see this predilection at work in his interpretations of Ida Bauer's dreams.

Another change in Freud's psychological instrumentarium was abandonment of the 'seduction theory'. At an early stage of his work with hysterics, he believed that their disturbances could all be traced back to premature sexual experience in childhood.[48]

---

[47] On these comparisons, see Malcolm Macmillan, *Freud Evaluated: The Completed Arc* (Cambridge, Mass.: MIT Press, 1997), 570–4.

[48] See 'The Aetiology of Hysteria' (1896), SE iii. 191–221.

In 1897, however, he found himself compelled to dismiss this theory. Practically, it did not help him in overcoming his patients' disorders, and realistically it seemed highly improbable that child-abuse was so very widespread as this theory demanded.[49] Freud has been much criticized for abandoning this theory, since the abuse of children was common in late-nineteenth-century Vienna, as elsewhere.[50] It is curious, however, that in his paper of 1896, 'The Aetiology of Hysteria', he attributed the premature sex sometimes to adults, whose relations with children might range from violent to consensual, and sometimes to other children, yet in writing to Fliess he claimed to have discovered that 'in all cases the *father*, not excluding my own, had to be accused of being perverse'.[51] Why does Freud, having identified a widespread practice of sexual interference with children, suddenly narrow it down to paternal abuse? Even if the seduction theory was a construction by Freud which he imposed on his patients, it is not clear why he changed from one to another version of it.[52] An explanation may be sought in the emotional turmoil into which Freud was thrown by the death of his father on 23 October 1896.[53]

In place of the seduction theory, Freud theorized that emotional disorders centring on sexual ideas were rooted in the internal structure of the psyche. The central arch of this structure was the famous 'Oedipus complex'. Although he does not use this as a technical term till 1910, he told his friend Fliess as early as 1897, only a month after giving up on the seduction theory,

[49] See Freud's letter of 21 Sept. 1897, in *Letters of Freud to Fliess*, 264–6.

[50] See Jeffrey Masson, *Freud: The Assault on Truth* (London: Faber, 1984); Larry Wolff, *Postcards from the End of the World: An Investigation into the Mind of Fin-de-siècle Vienna* (London: Collins, 1989).

[51] *Letters of Freud to Fliess*, 264. This discrepancy is discussed by Han Israëls, *Der Fall Freud: Die Geburt der Psychoanalyse aus der Lüge*, tr. Gerd Busse (Hamburg: Europäische Verlagsanstalt, 1999), p. 199.

[52] See Frank Cioffi, 'Was Freud a Liar?', in his *Freud and the Question of Pseudoscience* (Chicago and La Salle, Ill.: Open Court, 1998), 199–204.

[53] See Marianne Krüll, *Freud and his Father*, tr. Arnold J. Pomerans (London: Hutchinson, 1987); Marie Balmary, *Psychoanalyzing Psychoanalysis: Freud and the Hidden Fault of the Father*, tr. Ned Lukacher (Baltimore: Johns Hopkins University Press, 1982).

that the story of Oedipus expressed an emotional conflict common to all men:

I have found, in my own case too, [the phenomenon of] being in love with my mother and jealous of my father, and I now consider it a universal event in early childhood, even if not so early as in children who have been made hysterical. . . . If this is so, we can understand the gripping power of Oedipus Rex, in spite of all the objections that reason raises against the presupposition of fate. . . . Everyone in the audience was once a budding Oedipus in fantasy and each recoils in horror from the dream fulfilment here transplanted into reality, with the full quantity of repression which separates his infantile state from his present one.[54]

If the story of Oedipus provided a model for male psychosexual development, there had to be an equivalent model for female development. The little girl must be in love with her father, and feel her mother as a rival for his love. Hence it became essential to Freud's analysis of 'Dora' that she must be in love with her father, and he told her so very bluntly. On the other hand, the Oedipus complex allowed no space for the exploration of sibling relationships and rivalries, which may be why Freud does not discuss the relations between 'Dora' and her brother.[55]

Finally, Freud first formulates in this text the important concept of transference. The psychoanalytic patient unconsciously transfers onto the therapist positive or negative emotions that she has felt towards important people in her life. By realizing when transference is happening—when, for example, the patient displays unexpected affection or hostility—the therapist can gain access to earlier emotional experiences of the patient. What Freud does not say, and had not yet come to realize, is that in the highly charged atmosphere of the consulting-room there can also be counter-transference, in which the therapist projects past emotional experiences on to the patient, and this too can be either positive or negative. Towards the end of the case history Freud reproaches himself for failing to control his patient's transference.

[54] *Letters of Freud to Fliess*, 272. Cf. *The Interpretation of Dreams*, 201–4.

[55] Mitchell, *Mad Men and Medusas*, 106. On Freud's neglect of sibling relationships in general, see ibid. 23–7.

What perhaps prevented him, as we shall presently see, was his blindness towards his own feelings about her.

The reader will already have noticed that Freud's methods of interpretation allow considerable licence. All symptoms are over-determined and have multiple meanings: 'When you enter the field of psychoanalytical work, you very soon find out that a symptom has more than one meaning, and serves to present several unconscious thought processes at the same time' (p. 39). Apparent contradictions can be explained by the observation 'that ideas, even opposite ideas, live side by side without quarrelling particularly easily in the unconscious, and such a state of affairs often enough remains the same in the conscious mind' (p. 52). This, however, may be considered as a get-out-of-jail-free card which Freud keeps up his sleeve to justify apparent contradictions in his interpretation. Whether or not the unconscious can accommodate contradictions, Freud's theory certainly can.

The patient's opinions count for nothing; Freud's authority is all-powerful. Sceptical responses by the patient are construed as admissions, on the grounds that the unconscious cannot say 'No'.[56] Thus, when Freud tells his patient that a jewel-box of which she has dreamt signifies the female genitals, she replies, 'I knew *you* were going to say that,' which Freud interprets as an admission that *she* knew it (p. 59). There are, moreover, symptomatic actions by which patients betray themselves, but they cannot mislead the observant analyst. 'Those who have eyes to see and ears to hear will soon convince themselves that mortals cannot hide any secret. If our lips are sealed we talk volubly with our fingertips; we betray ourselves through every pore' (p. 66). 'This, we are forced to recall,' comments Steven Marcus, 'is from the Freud who more than anyone else in the history of Western civilization has taught us to be critically aware of fantasies of omniscience, and who on other occasions could be critical of such tendencies in himself. But not here where the demon of interpretation is riding him.'[57]

---

[56] Freud develops this claim in 'Negation' (1925), SE xix. 235–9.
[57] Marcus, 'Freud and Dora', 302.

Writing the Case History

Freud wrote up the case history early in January 1901, immediately after the abrupt conclusion of the treatment, but published it only in 1905. The reasons for this delay are unclear. He sent it to a journal, but had it rejected, probably because of the danger that 'Dora' and her family might be recognized; he then had it accepted by another journal, but withdrew it.[58] We do not know how much he revised it in the meantime, apart from adding footnotes, a preface, and an afterword. We do know, however, that Freud attached great importance to this text. He described it to Fliess as 'the subtlest thing I have written so far'.[59] Originally he intended to call it 'Dream and Hysteria', indicating that it would combine the findings of his studies on hysteria with his more recent work on dream-interpretation; it would also mention the concept of bisexuality, which Freud owed to Fliess, and which would later play an important role in the *Three Essays on the Theory of Sexuality* (1905). Thus, the account of Dora was intended as more than a case history; it was an important practical illustration of Freud's main theories.

Freud's case history has been much admired for its narrative skill. Dora's domestic situation is unveiled gradually. Freud presses further into her family secrets and into the secrets of her own psyche, drawing away successive veils of mystification, and disclosing unexpected correspondences between different incidents. Dora's symptoms and dreams turn out to be rich in intricately connected meanings. Sometimes these meanings centre on images which recur like literary leitmotifs, such as the box which occurs in Dora's dream and also appears as the reticule she plays with during the analysis. Edward Timms has suggested that the case history is structurally comparable to a novella, which often—though not as often as outdated theories of the novella used to claim—turns on a central symbol.[60] The falcon which

[58] See Ernest Jones, *Sigmund Freud: Life and Work*, 3 vols. (London: The Hogarth Press, 1953–7), ii. 286–7.

[59] *Letters of Freud to Fliess*, 433 (25 Jan. 1901).

[60] Edward Timms, 'Novelle and Case History: Freud in Pursuit of the Falcon', in *London German Studies II*, ed. J. P. Stern (London: Institute of Germanic Studies, 1983), 115–34 (p. 122).

unifies a novella by Boccaccio was taken up by nineteenth-century theorists who put forward the 'Falkentheorie' of the novella's construction. Within this web of interconnected images, the case history has the narrative thrust of a detective story, where narrative forward movement matters less than the detective's task of interpreting clues in order finally to disclose an unpredictable but conclusive meaning in what at first seemed an incoherent set of trivial events. At times, Freud's interpretation seems to click into place as neatly as the explanations given by Hercule Poirot at the end of an Agatha Christie mystery. Steven Marcus has made much bolder claims, arguing that the complexity of Freud's narrative anticipates the intricacy of a modernist novel:

The general form, then, of what Freud has written bears certain suggestive resemblances to a modern experimental novel. Its narrative and expository course, for example, is neither linear nor rectilinear; instead, its organization is plastic, involuted, and heterogeneous, and follows spontaneously an inner logic that seems frequently to be at odds with itself; it often loops back around itself and is multi-dimensional in its representation of both its material and itself. Its continuous innovations in formal structure seem unavoidably to be dictated by its substance, by the dangerous, audacious, disreputable, and problematical character of the experiences being represented and dealt with, and by the equally scandalous intentions of the author and the outrageous character of the role he has had the presumption to assume.[61]

To this we may add another layer of complexity. As one reads, especially at the distance of more than a century, one becomes suspicious of Freud's claims to narrative and interpretive authority. The text demands to be read against the grain, and Freud must be considered an unreliable narrator, whose judgements, and even many of his factual assertions, require constant alertness on the part of the reader. His use of free indirect speech can also mislead us by making the patient seem to report thoughts and motives which are actually attributed to her by Freud as analyst and narrator.[62]

[61] Marcus, 'Freud and Dora', 263–4.
[62] See Borch-Jacobsen and Shamdasani, *The Freud Files*, 205.

Freud himself was well aware that his case history resembled a work of fiction. He insists that it is not a 'Novelle' when he considers himself obliged to 'mention another complication, to which I certainly would not devote space if I were a writer inventing such a state of mind for a novella, instead of analysing it as a doctor' (p. 50). If we apply Freudian methods of interpretation to Freud himself, then this negation must be read as an affirmation. Freud is unwittingly acknowledging that what he has written contains at least a large measure of fiction.

Henceforth Freud's 'Fragment' will be treated as a work of the imagination—which does not mean something false or fabricated. Ida Bauer, Philipp Bauer, Katharina Bauer, and the Zellenkas will henceforth be called Dora, Dora's father and mother, and Herr and Frau K., the names they bear in Freud's text. To avoid describing as fact the events that Dora reported or Freud conjectured, the emphasis will be placed on Freud's construction and interpretation of the events reported by Dora. The present tense will be used for what happened in the consulting-room and for Freud's activity in writing the text; the past tense will be used for the events recounted or imagined there. The reader who has got this far should now stop reading the introduction and turn straight to Freud's text.

Dora and Herr K.

Freud assumes from the outset that Dora, as a hysteric, must be suffering from a trauma which is sexual in origin. On the surface, the trauma is obvious: it is the experience of receiving a sexual proposition from Herr K. in their fateful walk beside the lake. We may add, however, that Dora was distressed not only by this recollection, but by everyone's refusal to believe her account of it. Not only did Herr K. deny it outright, but he also told her father that, according to his wife, Dora was obsessed with sex and had read books about sex that the K.s had in their house. Yet by her own account, Dora and Frau K. had been intimate friends, while Herr K. had sent her flowers every day for a year (except when travelling) and had given her many expensive presents. Such a situation was indeed desperate, as Steven Marcus sums up:

> The three adults to whom she was closest, whom she loved the most in the world, were apparently conspiring—separately, in tandem, or in concert—to deny her the reality of her experience. They were conspiring to deny Dora her reality and reality itself. This betrayal touched upon matters that might easily unhinge the mind of a young person; for the three adults were not betraying Dora's love and trust alone, they were betraying the structure of the actual world.[63]

Dora is anxious to talk about her father's relationship with Frau K. Although her father had assured Freud that it was a 'genuine friendship' involving 'nothing wrong' (p. 21), Dora piles up evidence that they are lovers, telling, for example, how, when both families stayed in the hotel, her father and Frau K. managed to move to bedrooms opposite each other at the end of a corridor. When she protested to her mother, the latter told her that her father was grateful to Frau K. for having dissuaded him from committing suicide, a story that Dora does not believe.[64] Another piece of evidence Dora cites is that earlier Frau K. was unable to walk, not for organic reasons but from nervous paralysis which induced her to stay in a clinic, but that she made a full recovery when she started seeing a lot of Dora's father. This anecdote at least heightens the atmosphere of illness—much of it artificially induced—that hangs over the Bauer household.

It gets worse. Dora is convinced that her father has made a pact with Herr K. to hand her, Dora, over to him in return for his allowing her father to carry on the affair with Frau K. Freud's response to this accusation is curiously contorted. Although he accepts, by implication, that Dora's father is having an affair with Frau K. ('it was also easy to see in which particular accusation she was right': p. 28), and although he agrees with Dora's characterization of her father as dishonest, selfish, and self-deceiving, he states as a matter of fact that the men had made no such

[63] Marcus, 'Freud and Dora', 255–6.

[64] Dora's recourse to her mother, here and elsewhere, suggests that Frau Bauer was more important in Ida's life than Freud's text implies. See Mitchell, *Mad Men and Medusas*, 96–7.

agreement: 'Of course, the two men never concluded a formal agreement in which she was an object of barter' (p. 28). Moreover, he goes on to reconstruct the—illogical and self-deceiving—reasons with which Dora's father would have reassured himself. He would have known that his daughter was too reliable to be tempted by Herr K.'s advances, and anyway his friend was incapable of making such advances. This reconstruction of Dora's father's reasoning suggests that Freud does believe in an implicit understanding between him and Herr K. However, though he partially and indirectly acknowledges the betrayal that Dora believes she has suffered, he is not interested in pursuing the matter. Indeed, he cannot understand why she makes such a fuss about it.

What initially interests Freud is Dora's feelings for Herr K. He soon obtains from her an account of a still more traumatic experience that happened two years earlier, when Dora was thirteen.[65] Herr K. managed to get Dora alone in his shop, grabbed her, and kissed her on the lips. She felt a strong disgust, tore herself away, and ran out of the shop. This reaction confirms for Freud that Dora is a hysteric, because a normal girl would have felt sexually excited. It is therefore not Herr K.'s behaviour, but Dora's, that Freud disapproves of.[66]

The clue to Dora's reaction is given by her statement that she can still feel Herr K.'s pressure on her thorax or chest. Freud equates the sensation of external pressure with a sensation she must have felt inside her body, on the grounds that disgust is a sensation appropriate to the throat and the digestive tract. He also surmises that Dora must really have felt an uncomfortable sensation lower down, from Herr K.'s erect penis pressing against her, and in her memory has transferred the sensation from her lower to her upper body. By a cunning sleight of hand, Freud transfers the sensation one step further, from the exterior of Dora's body to the interior.

[65] Freud mistakenly says 'fourteen' (p. 22), possibly to palliate the account, since fourteen was the age of consent in Austria at this time: Leo A. Lensing, review of Decker's *Freud, Dora, and Vienna*, *Austrian Studies*, 3 (1992), 176–9 (p. 179).

[66] See Madelon Sprengnether, 'Enforcing Oedipus: Freud and Dora', in Bernheimer and Kahane (eds.), *In Dora's Case*, 254–75 (p. 259).

Later in the analysis Freud returns to Dora's alleged disgust and offers another explanation for it. What Dora really found disgusting was her own vaginal emission. Having been told by her governess that all men were untrustworthy, Dora, knowing of her father's illness, understood this to mean that all men were sexually diseased, which for her meant afflicted with a catarrhal emission. She therefore projected her own feeling of self-disgust on to men, above all on to Herr K. when he embraced her. So her revulsion against his embrace, which for Freud is a riddle needing to be solved, was not due to a thirteen-year-old girl's fright at being suddenly seized by a grown man, nor to her fear that the man might be diseased (since she had no realistic conception of a man's venereal disease), but arose from her disgust with her own body and its emissions, which she projected on to Herr K.

Although Dora tore herself loose from Herr K. and ran away the first time he assailed her, and slapped his face the second time, Freud is convinced that she must be in love with him. One piece of evidence is Dora's dislike for the governess who she thought was in love with her father and therefore only paid attention to her when her father was around. Freud maintains that the governess's behaviour was analogous to Dora's. The governess looked after Dora only as a way of being near her father. Dora looked after the K.s' children, but only as a means of getting close to Herr K. Further evidence comes from the fact that Dora's bouts of aphonia lasted from three to six weeks, and Herr K.'s absences on business also lasted three to six weeks (a period too elastic, one would think, to permit the analogy). When she had aphonia, she wrote instead of speaking; Freud points out that when a beloved person is away, one writes to him because one cannot speak to him, and takes this as proof that her aphonia symbolized her distress at Herr K.'s absence. Admittedly, her aphonia did not coincide in time, only in duration, with Herr K.'s absences, but that is explained as an unconscious deception intended to hide the relationship.

Further evidence that Dora loves Herr K. is found in her first dream, in which her father wakes her because of a fire, and her mother wants to save a jewel-box. As a dream never means what its surface elements suggest, Freud decodes the dream via a dizzy-ingly complicated series of reversals and substitutions. The easiest of these is supplied by Dora's recollection of how, on the after-noon following the incident beside the lake, she fell asleep on the sofa and awoke to find Herr K. standing before her. So in the dream Dora has substituted her father for Herr K.

After that, the interpretation becomes much more elaborate. Dora recollects that her father gave her mother a bracelet which the latter rejected, and that Herr K. gave her a jewel-box which she accepted. In the dream, it appears, Dora has replaced her mother with herself and Herr K. with her father, and instead of Herr K. giving her a jewel-box, she wants to give him her jewel-box. And since the jewel-box clearly symbolizes the female geni-tals, the dream is Dora's admission of her desire for Herr K. Her fear of fire attests the intensity of her attraction to Herr K. and her fear of her own weakness in yielding to it. 'You are thus confirm-ing', Freud concludes triumphantly, 'how intense your love for him was' (p. 59).

Supplementary evidence is found in Dora's later recollection that after waking from this dream she could smell smoke. Freud connects this with the fact that Herr K., like Dora's father and indeed Freud himself, was a heavy smoker. Since Dora supplies this recollection only after some delay, it must correspond to something deeply repressed and therefore important. This repressed content must be the kiss that Herr K. forced on her and which would have tasted of smoke. It is a further indication that her love for Herr K. is so intense that her unconscious has to work hard to repress it.

The analysis of Dora's second dream supplies Freud with even more compelling evidence of Dora's love for Herr K. Dora tells Freud how she had an apparent attack of appendicitis, with high fever, abdominal pains, and constipation. Freud wishes to inter-pret this attack as hysterical, but is at first unsure how to justify this interpretation. When he asks about its timing, however, he learns that it took place exactly nine months after Herr K. propos-itioned her beside the lake. Now all is clear. Dora was imitating childbirth and fantasizing that she was bearing Herr K.'s child.

Moreover, after her hysterical appendicitis she dragged one foot; this was not due to organic lameness, in Freud's view, but symbolized her feeling that she had made a 'Fehltritt' or false step—that is, in relation to Herr K.

A fantasy of pregnancy also appears behind the image of the Madonna, though this is not actually in Dora's dream.[67] The strange city in the dream recalls Dresden, which Dora has visited, and where she spent two hours looking at the *Sistine Madonna*.[68] Freud adds in a footnote that when girls are accused of sexual misdemeanours, they often respond by resorting to the counter-image of the pure Virgin, and that Dora, besides being in this situation, identified herself with the Madonna through the fantasy of having a child while retaining her virginity. One might have expected, though, that if Dora spent two hours in front of this picture, its importance for her emotional life might have merited more from Freud than a hasty footnote. Mary Jacobus has perceptively related Freud's lack of interest in this image to his tendency to write off Dora's mother and to underrate mothers in general. She asks provocatively: 'what does it mean to be a mother when mothers are the waste product of a sexual system based on the exchange of women among men?'[69]

Freud's prepossession in favour of Herr K. becomes increasingly clear. Early in the text he observes in a footnote that Herr K.'s approach to Dora beside the lake was 'by no means crude or offensive', and that her rejection of him was 'brutal' (p. 31). He mentions in another footnote that he has met Herr K., and that the latter is 'a still youthful man of attractive appearance' (p. 23).

[67] An example of how commentators over-enthusiastically accept Freud's interpretations: 'The Madonna found her way into Ida Bauer's dream precisely because she represented the negation of the "primal scene"—the negation of masculinity and femininity': Maria Ramas, 'Freud's Dora, Dora's Hysteria', in Bernheimer and Kahane (eds.), *In Dora's Case*, 149–80 (p. 173). Yet the Madonna is present only in Freud's interpretation of the dream, not in the dream itself.
[68] Reproduced and discussed by Mary Jacobus, '*Dora* and the Pregnant Madonna', in her *Reading Woman: Essays in Feminist Criticism* (London: Methuen, 1986), 137–93 (pp. 137–41).
[69] Ibid. 142. On Freud's lack of interest in Dora's mother, see also Toril Moi, 'Representation of Patriarchy: Sexuality and Epistemology in Freud's Dora', in Bernheimer and Kahane (eds.), *In Dora's Case*, 181–99 (pp. 193–4).

In the course of the analysis, Freud becomes convinced that Herr K.'s approach to Dora was serious and honourable, and 'had not been an idle attempt at seduction' (p. 81).

So why did Dora slap Herr K. and run away? All is explained when the story of the K.s' governess comes to light. While staying with the K.s in the Alpine resort, Dora noticed that the governess who looked after their children treated Herr K. very disrespectfully. She found out that Herr K. had seduced this governess and had a brief affair with her, then abandoned her. The governess was angry, but instead of giving her notice immediately, she was staying on in the hope that Herr K. would relent towards her. The term of notice is usually two weeks. That is the length of time that Dora waited before telling her parents about Herr K.'s approach to her. So she was acting like the governess, and, like her, delaying telling her parents in the hope that Herr K. would renew his advances. When she did tell her parents, her motive was to take revenge on Herr K. for not doing so. This confirms Freud's earlier suspicion that in telling her parents about it she was taking revenge.

We may, however, attach more significance than Freud does to the timing of Dora's discovery about the K.s' governess. A few days before the incident by the lake, the governess told Dora that Herr K. had seduced her and mentioned that he had appealed to her by saying that 'there was nothing between him and his wife' (p. 90). These were the very words that Herr K. used to Dora when he offered a sexual relationship. It would not take much worldly wisdom to recognize in these repeated words a routine appeal made by a practised seducer.

Freud, unlike Dora, seems blind to Herr K.'s most likely intentions. As Dora knows that the K.s often discussed divorce, Freud suggests to her that she was hoping that Herr K. would divorce his wife and marry her. Moreover, Freud thinks that Dora had a serious plan to marry Herr K., and that as Herr K. was serious in his intentions towards her, this would have been an excellent outcome. That explains why she was so indignant at having her story disbelieved. She was really indignant, not about that, but at being disappointed in her hopes of marrying Herr K. So Freud's account of the matter is that Herr K. was an honourable man who made a serious proposition to Dora, involving divorcing his wife and marrying her. Dora wanted this to happen, but being a hysteric, she was her own worst enemy: she rejected his proposition, then was angry with him for not renewing it and took revenge on him by telling her parents. So Dora is responsible for ruining her own life.

Dora and her Father

Freud also spends a lot of time proving that Dora is in love with her father. He is puzzled by her anger at being disbelieved. He cannot take it at face value. There must be something behind it, because one does not get so upset over an unfounded accusation. If she was not lying, she should not have been so upset at being called a liar. No, she must be responding to a hidden self-reproach, a nerve which the disbelief has struck. He finds the clue in Dora's incessant cough. He ascribes it to her identification with her father. When she alleges that Frau K. loves her father only because he is prosperous ('a man of means'), Freud deduces that she really means the opposite, i.e. that he is impotent. Dora confirms this 'as something of which she was aware' (p. 39); Freud never wonders how she knows. In that case, Freud continues, her father's intercourse with Frau K. must be oral, and Dora unconsciously knows it. This unconscious knowledge is symbolized by her cough, which produces a sensation in her throat analogous to the sensation produced by her father's penis in Frau K.'s throat. She was in any case predisposed towards oral sex by her early habit of sucking her thumb.

Commentators on the case of Dora have been keen to assert that, rather than being fellated by Frau K., Dora's father must have practised cunnilingus with her. Thus Jacques Lacan declared that Freud had no need to invoke fellatio, 'when everyone knows that cunnilingus is the artifice most commonly adopted by "men of means" whose powers begin to abandon them'.[70] However, the

---

[70] Jacques Lacan, 'Intervention on Transference', tr. Jacqueline Rose, in Bernheimer and Kahane (eds.), *In Dora's Case*, 92–104 (p. 98). 'It is hard to guess what Freud would have made of this note of high Parisian *savoir vivre*': Neil Hertz, 'Dora's Secrets, Freud's

point is not what Dora's father and Frau K. did together, but what Freud imagined them doing, and what fantasies about their intercourse he imputed to Dora. And it may well show Freud's overvaluation of phallic sexuality that a form of intercourse not involving the penis, in which the man appeared subordinate and worked at giving pleasure to the woman, did not occur to him as a possibility.

Further evidence for Dora's love for her father is that her strong feelings about his relationship with Frau K. are, in Freud's view, excessive or disproportionate. They must conceal another, contrary feeling. That feeling is her own love for her father. She is indignant at the relationship because she would like to be in Frau K.'s place, and she puts herself in that place symbolically by her cough, thus imagining her father's penis in her mouth. Freud concludes bluntly 'that she was in love with her father' (p. 47). When he tells her so, she replies: 'I don't remember,' and offers a reminiscence about a cousin (who, when her parents were quarrelling, said she hated her mother) which serves Freud as an indirect admission. The unconscious cannot say 'No'; there is no negation there. So she isn't in love with Herr K. after all, then? Oh yes she is—the love for her father is simply a reaction symptom, summoned up in order to conceal from herself that she is still really in love with Herr K.

Freud's desire to prove that Dora is in love with her father may explain his extraordinary anxiety to establish that she masturbated as a child. He arrives at this (in itself unremarkable) conclusion by analysing Dora's first dream. Her father saves her from a fire. By the dream-work's technique of reversal, fire represents water, and water represents Dora's memory of wetting her bed. So the underlying dream-thought was that she wanted her father to save her, not from a fire, but from a wet bed. Freud now tells us that since Dora not only wetted her bed as a child, but resumed doing so at about the age of eight, this renewed bed-wetting must be the result of masturbation, which, in Freud's view, plays a hitherto underestimated role in the aetiology of bed-wetting.

Techniques', in ibid. 221–42 (p. 228). Cf. Roy Porter, *A Social History of Madness: Stories of the Insane* (London: Weidenfeld & Nicolson, 1987), 114.

Her masturbation is further proved by the fact that one day in the analysis she has a fashionable purse with her and keeps opening it, inserting a finger, and closing it again. Freud interprets this as a symptomatic action that symbolizes masturbation.

But why is Freud so keen to prove that Dora used to masturbate? Dora tells him that her mother received a venereal infection from her father, and went to Franzensbad in the hope of alleviating it. Freud asks Dora straight out if she too has a venereal illness, and is told that she, like her mother, has a vaginal discharge. Freud now concludes that in accusing her father of infecting her, she is really accusing herself of something. He tells her that when girls have such a discharge, the main cause is usually masturbation, and that all other causes are trivial by comparison. It is not clear whether Freud includes venereal infection among these trivial causes, but at any rate he is either minimizing, or denying, her father's responsibility for her ailment, and thus transferring the main responsibility for her illness to Dora herself. Her discharge results from her early masturbation, and her unconscious is guiltily aware of it.

Freud's attitude is difficult to identify. There were still many moralists and doctors who warned that masturbators risked consumption, convulsions, epilepsy, a bent spine, amnesia, and idiocy.[71] Although Freud did not go to such lengths, he described masturbation as 'wrong-doing' and considered it a major cause of neurasthenia.[72] He knew too that masturbation was as common among women as among men. His anxiety to prove that Dora masturbated makes him sound like a prosecutor intent on finding evidence of depravity.

At the same time, masturbation was coming to play an important role in Freud's theory of sexual development. Some years previously he had attributed hysteria to seduction in early childhood. Having abandoned the seduction theory, he was now seeking to replace it with a theory of early masturbation as the cause of hysteria. The unfocused erotic energy of early childhood is turned

---

[71] Gay, *Bourgeois Experience*, i. 300.

[72] SE iii. 55; as cause of neurasthenia, SE iii. 275, xii. 251. See 'A Discussion on Masturbation: Concluding Remarks' (1912), SE xii. 243–54.

by the masturbator into self-indulgent fantasy which alienates one from reality and helps to generate hysteria.[73]

The theme of masturbation evidently gets Freud excited and sends him off at a tangent. He tells us that masturbators often suffer from abdominal pains—though this is true of women afflicted with gonorrhoea, and if Freud shared the belief, widespread in his day, that sexual diseases could be inherited, this might have suggested itself as a more likely explanation, if Freud had not been so keen to exonerate Dora's father from responsibility for her illness. This reminds Freud of the eccentric theories about the relation between the nose and other parts of the body upheld by his Berlin colleague and confidant Wilhelm Fliess. Freud's attachment to Fliess not only led him, at least temporarily, to accept these theories, but also to put them into practice in the treatment of one of his hysterical patients, Emma Eckstein. Thinking her hysteria was sexual in origin, and accepting Fliess's claim of a link between the nose and the genitals, Freud induced Fliess to operate on Eckstein's nose. The result was a near-fatal haemorrhage which turned out to have been caused by Fliess leaving half-a-metre of gauze in the patient's nasal cavity. Instead of criticizing Fliess's incompetence, Freud downplayed it by telling him that the patient's nosebleeds were really hysterical in origin, an attempt to obtain her doctor's love.[74] We see here the solidarity among men, and the tendency to blame the victim, which are prominent also in the story of Dora. In her case, Freud tells us that according to Fliess stomach-pains can be treated by finding a spot in the nose that is connected to the stomach and applying cocaine to it. Here, comments Steven Marcus, we 'are in the positive presence of demented and delusional science'.[75]

Freud then returns to Dora's masturbation and asks why she gave it up. For reasons which he does not specify, but sums up as

---

[73] See Thomas Laqueur, *Solitary Sex: A Cultural History of Masturbation* (New York: Zone Books, 2003), 387–93.

[74] *Letters of Freud to Fliess*, 186 (4 May 1896). On the Eckstein affair, see Masson, *The Assault on Truth*, 55–72. For a full account of Fliess's theories, see Frank J. Sulloway, *Freud, Biologist of the Mind: Beyond the Psychoanalytic Legend*, 2nd edn. (Cambridge, Mass., and London: Harvard University Press, 1992), 135–70.

[75] Marcus, 'Freud and Dora', 302.

'symptomatic actions and other signs' (p. 68), Freud has 'good grounds to assume' that as a child Dora slept in a bedroom next to her parents' bedroom and that she overheard her father having intercourse with her mother. She knew her father suffered from asthma, and when she heard him panting, she was afraid the overexertion would harm him. Knowing quite well why he was panting, she associated this sound with her own panting induced by her masturbatory orgasms. So she gave up masturbating for fear of injuring herself, and, as a means of identifying with her father, began to suffer from difficulties of breathing which were psychosomatic in origin.

But it doesn't end there. Dora also feels jealousy over Frau K. and a homosexual attraction to her. Previously, Dora shared a bedroom with Frau K. and was her confidante. She speaks enthusiastically to Freud about Frau K.'s 'enchantingly white body'. Some readers have made much of the putative relationship between Dora and Frau K. 'It seems quite clear', says Maria Ramas, 'that the intimate sexual discussions that occupied so much of Ida and Frau K.'s time alone together had erotic meaning to them both.'[76] Without exaggerating the closeness between the two women (Dora says they shared a bedroom, not a bed), Ramas imagines them enjoying an intense emotional intimacy by sharing heterosexual fantasies, which served to mask the homosexual desires that were thus finding indirect satisfaction. Or, for all we know, Dora may have been consciously homosexual but concealed the fact from Freud, as Hélène Cixous affirms.[77] Patrick Mahony surmises, though with notable uncertainty, that Dora's psychosomatic coughing, which Freud thinks symbolizes her identification with Frau K. fellating her father, instead symbolizes her own repressed fantasy of herself practising cunnilingus with

---

[76] Ramas, 'Freud's Dora, Dora's Hysteria', 164.

[77] Hélène Cixous and Catherine Clément, *The Newly Born Woman*, tr. Betsy Wing (Manchester: Manchester University Press, 1986), 48–9. Appignanesi and Forrester support this interpretation (*Freud's Women*, 152, 156). But cf. the critical reservations expressed by Moi, 'Representation of Patriarchy', 192, and this sober reflection: 'Dora obviously worshipped Mrs. K., but one naturally wonders how much of Mrs. K.'s attachment was heartfelt and how much sprang from a desire to be on good terms with her lover's daughter' (Decker, *Freud, Dora, and Vienna*, 68).

Frau K.: 'Over time Dora's coughing would have appeared to acquire the meaning of cunnilingus with Peppina.'[78]

Without pursuing these speculative routes, one may note Freud's uncertainty about love between women. Near the end of Part 1, Freud downplays Dora's putative feelings for Frau K. by saying they typify the unconscious homosexual feelings of hysterical girls. In other words, they are what we might call a schoolgirl crush. Only in a late footnote added to the text, and using a strange word, does he admit the possibility of a 'gynaecophile' relationship (p. 103). Yet while he was analysing Dora, he was also treating a woman, known only as Frau L.G., whom he considered 'at a deeper level gynecophilic [*sic*]'.[79] The possibility of love between women must have been present to his mind, but he has difficulty in admitting that such feelings exist.

Here Freud introduces a puzzling classical allusion to which commentators have paid little attention. Talking about the close relationship between Dora and Frau K., he abruptly says: 'Medea was happy for Creusa to make friends with her two children as well, and she certainly did nothing to disturb their father's contact with the girl' (p. 51). The allusion is to Euripides' *Medea* and to the modernized version by the classic nineteenth-century Austrian dramatist Franz Grillparzer, with whose work Freud often shows himself to be familiar. Medea, the 'barbaric' princess of Colchis, is living in Corinth as the wife of Jason, and is for a time friendly with the Corinthian princess Creusa; but when Jason resolves to discard Medea and marry Creusa, Medea kills her rival and also her own children. This deed has always made Medea an especially problematic tragic heroine.[80] An allusion to it, which the mention of Medea cannot fail to evoke, seems altogether excessive. In the analogy, Medea corresponds to Frau K.,

---

[78] Mahony, *Freud's Dora*, p. 28. Note the uncertainty signalled by Mahony's 'would have' instead of 'did'; the ambiguity of 'appeared', which may mean 'probably acquired' or '[only] seemed to acquire'. And if the cough was not originally a meaningful symptom, why and how did it subsequently 'acquire' meaning? This uncertainty is characteristic of commentators who perceive the extravagance of Freud's reasoning but want to shore up the Freudian framework.

[79] *Letters of Freud to Fliess*, 406 (23 Mar. 1900).

[80] See Edith Hall, *Greek Tragedy: Suffering under the Sun* (Oxford: Oxford University Press, 2010), 242–5.

and Creusa to Dora, who helps to look after the children. The most obvious function of the reference to Medea and Creusa is to suggest that the friendship between Frau K. and Dora was temporary and superficial, and to imply a latent but much more powerful antagonism, so that the possibility of love between two women is negated. It may also imply that Freud is suspicious of Frau K. and even thinks her capable of such a monstrous deed as infanticide; when he published the case history, he knew that in the meantime Frau K.'s sickly daughter had died.

Dora and Freud

Freud often seems uncertain about how grown-up Dora is. In his account of events, he gets her age wrong by saying that she was fourteen, instead of thirteen, when Herr K. kissed her in his shop. Even at the time of her treatment by Freud, she is variously described as a child and a girl. This may remind us of the ambiguity surrounding female children in some nineteenth-century novels, such as Henry James's *What Maisie Knew* (1897), a book almost contemporary with the case of Dora. It is hard to make out how old Maisie is at any point in the book—eight? ten? fourteen?—and how much she knows about the sordid machinations going on among the adults who surround her. We can only be sure that she apprehends much more than she—or the narrator on her behalf—can put into words.[81]

In keeping with his uncertainty about Dora's maturity, a recurrent and very pressing issue for Freud is the extent and source of Dora's sexual knowledge. He seems on the one hand to assume that she knows, or at least should know, very little. He tells us that he is at pains to avoid telling her more about sex than she knows already, though when he does talk about sexual matters he uses frank language. Whenever a sexual topic is raised, Dora says that she didn't know it in the past, but knows it now, though she doesn't know how she knows. Freud concludes that she learnt much from Frau K., though he places this conclusion only in a

---

[81] See Sally Shuttleworth, *The Mind of the Child: Child Development in Literature, Science, and Medicine, 1840–1900* (Oxford: Oxford University Press, 2010), 325–34.

footnote near the end of the text and reproaches himself for not guessing it sooner (p. 103). He does not pursue the allegation, reported by Dora's father as coming from Herr K. and to him from Frau K., that at the K.s' house Dora read Paolo Mantegazza's *Physiology of Love* and similar books. While *The Physiology of Love* has been described as mainly 'a romantic and sentimental paen [sic] to human reproduction', other books by Mantegazza, such as *The Sexual Relations of Mankind*, would have informed Dora about many 'perversions', including various lesbian practices.[82] Mantegazza, a famous Italian neurologist and proponent of Darwinism, was in any case just one representative of a very extensive body of writing on sexology, ranging from the scientific to the popular, which was readily available, and—judging from the many impressions some works went through—widely read.[83]

Freud also fingers Dora's governess, described as 'an older and very well-read young woman' (p. 29), so presumably in her early twenties. (As the governess was still employed when the family were living in Reichenberg, she must have been looking after Dora when the latter was sixteen or even older.) This governess, whom one would like to know much more about, apparently had 'liberal views' (p. 29) and read many books about sex and discussed them with Dora, while warning her to conceal the knowledge thus acquired from her parents. Dora further reports that the governess not only knew about the affair between Dora's father and Frau K. but urged Dora's mother and Dora herself to put a stop to it. Dora, however—again by her own account—was still very fond of Frau K., found nothing wrong in her relationship with her father, but concluded that the governess herself was in love with

---

[82] Sprengnether, 'Enforcing Oedipus', 273; Gilman, *The Jew's Body*, 89–90.

[83] A very long list of sexological authors, including 'S. Freud', is given in Iwan Bloch, *Das Sexualleben unserer Zeit in seinen Beziehungen zur modernen Kultur* (Berlin: Louis Marcus Verlagsbuchhandlung, 1909), 820. This is described as the 7th to 9th impression, with a print-run of 20,000, following 40,000 copies in previous impressions; it was first published in 1907. Before and after, Bloch, sometimes using the pseudonym 'Eugen Dühren', published many other studies on sexuality, some of which were translated into English. On the sexological literature of the turn of the century, see Anna Katharina Schaffner, *Modernism and Perversion* (Basingstoke: Palgrave Macmillan, 2012).

Dora's father and cared much more about him than about Dora, whereupon she insisted on the governess's dismissal.

Dora's second dream provides Freud with ample evidence of her sexual knowledge. She dreams that she is lost in a strange town and asks someone the way to the station. In discussion, she recollects asking her mother the whereabouts of a box which contained an album of city views. So the question 'Where is the station?' can be translated into 'Where is the box?' The album had sexual associations, since it was given to her by a young engineer who was thought to be a prospective suitor. Her questioning also calls to mind how she asked her inattentive mother repeatedly for a certain key. Questions about a key and a box are readily decoded as questions about the male and female genitals respectively.

In part of the dream Dora enters a dense forest. Superficially, this recalls the wood beside the lake where Herr K. propositioned her. Symbolically, Freud associates the forest with pubic hair. Since the dream already contains the explicit words *Bahnhof* (station) and *Friedhof* (cemetery), he thinks they disguise the presence of another compound noun ending in *-hof*, namely *Vorhof*, which can mean the vulval vestibule, an area at the entrance to the vagina. Questioned about the forest, Dora recollects going to the Secessionist exhibition and seeing a painting of a forest inhabited by nymphs. These nymphs must stand for 'nymphae', a medical term for the labia minora. So the dream, as Freud triumphantly observes, is a symbolic sexual geography. What it conceals is a fantasy of defloration. Dora has imagined her own genitals being penetrated by a man. The difficulty in moving that she felt in part of the dream represents both her own fear of penetration and the man's difficulty in penetrating her hymen. And the man, of course, must be Herr K.

This interpretation, however, intensifies the puzzle over Dora's sexual knowledge. Anyone who uses such technical terms as 'vestibule' and 'nymphae', Freud says, must have got them out of anatomical books or encyclopedias—regardless of the fact that it is not Dora but he who has used these terms. Dora now supplies another dream, or another part of the same dream, in which she quietly reads a large book. The large book, according to Freud, must be an encyclopedia or anatomical textbook in which she found out about sexual anatomy. Dora admits that when a cousin of hers had appendicitis, she read about appendicitis in an encyclopedia; Freud is sure that she also read about sex but has repressed the memory.[84] However, her recollection of reading 'quietly' is puzzling. According to Freud, people who surreptitiously consult encyclopedias to learn about sex do not read quietly or calmly, but in constant fear in case their parents come in and catch them at their forbidden reading. If Dora dreamt of reading quietly, therefore, that was because in her dream her father was dead and the rest of the family had gone to the cemetery to bury him. So she could read about sex without fear of interruption, which is to say, she could do it without being forbidden by her father.

On the other hand, Freud often assumes that sexual knowledge is very widespread and easily obtained. He thinks that children, including Dora, often learn about sex by overhearing their parents having intercourse, and know semi-consciously what is happening: 'In such cases, children guess at the sexual element in these strange sounds' (p. 68). He assumes that Dora knows, and has known for some time, enough about sexual intercourse to be aware that the man transmits a fluid to the woman, and that this fluid can be the means of venereal infection; this knowledge is supposed to underlie the theme of bed-wetting which Freud finds in her first dream, concealed by the imagery of fire. She is also supposed to have known that people who do not have sexual intercourse are bad sleepers, and that this was why her father slept badly after giving up sexual relations with his wife. He says the milder sexual perversions are extremely common among the population, so it is easy to learn about them. Hence Dora could easily know about the practice of fellatio. When he surmises that Dora's father is impotent, Dora confirms it; Freud does not wonder how she knows, but if she did say this, the obvious informant would be her

---

[84] Anthony Stadlen has examined the various popular encyclopedias available to Dora in 1899 and found that the word 'Vorhof' never occurs and 'Nymphen' only fleetingly: Stadlen, 'Was Dora "Ill"?', in Laurence Spurling (ed.), *Sigmund Freud: Critical Assessments*, 4 vols. (London and New York: Routledge, 1989), ii. 196–203 (p. 199).

mother, whom Freud never considers as a possible source of sexual knowledge.[85]

It is also important what *kind* of sexual knowledge is possessed. The kind of knowledge that Freud imputes to Dora, to other women, to children, and to large sections of the population, is secretive, exciting, and disturbing. It is acquired surreptitiously by children who overhear their parents having sex, by teenagers hastily consulting encyclopedias, and by women like Dora and Frau K. who have thrillingly intimate conversations in a shared bedroom. Freud also deplores the prurience with which sexual matters are commonly discussed and to which 'women and girls' are well used (p. 40). Such knowledge is not only *about* the erotic but is itself erotic. Freud, on the other hand, aspires to a knowledge about sex which is not sexually exciting. This kind of knowledge is scientific and expressed in the appropriate neutral language.[86] Hence, Freud insists that he takes care not to give Dora any sexual knowledge she did not already possess, nor to speak of sexual matters in erotic terms, but to call a spade a spade. Yet when he describes his practice of plain speaking, what he says is: 'J'appelle un chat un chat' (p. 41). He drops into French again a paragraph later when he says: 'Pour faire une omelette il faut casser des oeufs'. As for direct references to sexual practices, whatever plain terms he may have used to Dora, he thinks it necessary to spare the reader's sensibilities by referring to oral intercourse as 'sexual satisfaction *per os*'.[87] It is easy to imagine that, despite his attitude of clinical detachment, Freud, without admitting it, was sexually excited by his conversations with Dora. Some readers have gone further and maintained that in these analytic sessions Freud was unwittingly re-creating the

---

[85] See Moi, 'Representation of Patriarchy', 193.

[86] See Appignanesi and Forrester, *Freud's Women*, 158.

[87] Freud adopts the decent obscurity of a classical language not only in other publications, as when the Wolf Man is said to have seen his parents practising coitus *a tergo* ('from behind', SE xvii. 37), but even in private correspondence, as when he tells Fliess that at the age of two he saw *matrem nudam* ('his mother naked') and that a patient saw his nurse *podice nudo* ('with bare buttocks'): *Letters of Freud to Fliess*, 268 (3 Oct. 1897), 218 (17 Dec. 1896). Contrast the frankness he recommends in 'On the Sexual Enlightenment of Children' (1907), SE ix. 131–9.

erotic conversations he imagined taking place between Dora and Frau K., and thus implicitly placing himself in the position of a woman.[88]

Freud's account of Dora repeatedly implies that Dora has no authentic feelings of her own. Her 'show of wishing to commit suicide' was not only unserious: it was an imitation of the alleged suicide attempt by her father, even though she did not believe her father had made any such attempt (p. 27). As we have already seen, even one of the feelings that Dora expresses most strongly, her anger at being disbelieved, does not convince Freud. He cannot see why she goes on about it at such length. It must be a proxy for a hidden and more important feeling, namely her love for her father. Her illnesses too are not her own. It is not just that they are psychosomatic, though Freud never asks whether they might have an organic origin and never asks what previous doctors have said. They are not even her own psychosomatic illnesses: they are even more inauthentic, in that they are copied. When she has abdominal pains, Freud accuses her of copying a female cousin whom Dora considers to have manufactured her symptoms— so Dora is simulating a simulator. Her aphonia, as we have seen, is interpreted as symbolizing her distress at Herr K.'s absence. Her difficulty in breathing is supposed to have originated as an imitation of her father's panting during sexual intercourse. Freud admittedly does not claim that hysterical symptoms are *purely* manufactured; there has to be a 'somatic compliance' (p. 33). There is an organic stimulus, which is like the grain of sand round which a pearl forms in an oyster. Thus, her cough had a slight organic cause, but it was also an imitation of her tubercular father, expressing her identification with him and proclaiming that he had made her ill. Not only Dora's emotions, but even her physical symptoms, confirm her helpless dependence on men.

Freud, on the other hand, identifies with several of the men who figure in the Dora narrative. He identifies with Dora's father in telling her how much her father loves her and how she is

---

[88] Appignanesi and Forrester, *Freud's Women*, 159.

simulating illness to achieve purposes of her own or, failing that, to take revenge. In many surprising ways he identifies with Herr K., acquiring the increasingly strong conviction that the latter's intentions towards Dora were honourable, and expressing perplexity (which Herr K. himself may not have felt) at Dora's rejection of his advances.[89]

Freud ascribes transference to Dora, but not to himself. When she remembers the smell of smoke, he thinks this shows not only that she liked the smoky kiss she received from Herr K., but also that during the treatment she would like Freud, another smoker, to kiss her. Thus she is transferring on to Freud her (supposed) feelings for Herr K. One might wonder, however, whether a patient's feelings for her analyst really need to be understood as being transferred from another relationship and hence only apparently directed at the analyst. Why cannot the patient, especially in the emotionally charged atmosphere of the consulting-room, feel a real and strong attraction to the analyst, or an equally real and strong dislike?

It is certainly clear from the text that Freud does not like Dora.[90] He mentions that for several days she identified herself with her mother, that is, behaved like her mother—though as Freud never met her mother, he knows only from second-hand reports how she behaves—and thus treated Freud to 'the most impossible behaviour' (p. 64). He frequently accuses Dora of vindictiveness. Her 'brutal' rejection of Herr K.'s supposedly sincere advances is ascribed to revenge. In her second dream, the idea that her father is dead is interpreted as a fantasy of revenge against him. And of course her breaking-off of the analysis is an act of revenge against Freud. At the end, he tells how Dora paid him a visit some fifteen months later, and how her manner made it clear to him that she had ended the analysis in order to deny him the satisfaction of curing her completely. By imputing to her such a contorted and implausible motive, Freud betrays that his account

---

[89] On Freud's intermittent adoption of Herr K.'s viewpoint, see Philip McCaffrey, *Freud and Dora: The Artful Dream* (New Brunswick, NJ: Rutgers University Press, 1984), 91–3.

[90] A point made particularly forcefully by Mahony, *Freud's Dora*, 39–40.

of transference 'is being written by an angry man seeking justification'.[91]

Freud is throughout anxious to exclude the passage of emotions between himself as analyst and Dora as patient. If emotions appear, they must be transferred from another setting, not generated in the clinically pure environment of the consulting-room. Thus, the hygienic neutrality of the doctor–patient relationship is preserved.[92] In fact, however, Freud has included enough dramatic dialogue in his account (without claiming that it is an exact transcription of what they said) to show that the atmosphere was strained. Freud commandingly imposes his interpretations on Dora, while she replies either sceptically ('I knew *you* were going to say that', p. 59) or with indifference, as when she greets his triumphant interpretation of her second dream with the disparaging question: 'What came of all that?' (p. 89).

What attitude towards his patient, finally, does Freud imply by giving her the pseudonym 'Dora'? He himself says, in *The Psychopathology of Everyday Life*, that he was borrowing the name that had been given to Rosa, the nursemaid of his sister, also called Rosa, to avoid confusion between the two (SE vi. 241). To name her after a servant might be thought disparaging. Commentators have suggested other unconscious and also disparaging sources: the 'child-wife' Dora in Dickens's *David Copperfield*, or the Empress Theodora, whom Freud, when in Paris fifteen years earlier, had seen acted by Sarah Bernhardt in Victorien Sardou's play *Théodora*.[93] A possible mythological source is Pandora, whose curiosity made her open the box entrusted to her by her husband and thus unleash an array of evils upon the world. Janet Malcolm makes this suggestion on the grounds that the case history contains many references to boxes, and surmises that Freud was so hostile to Dora because he saw her 'as Original Woman, in all her beauty and evil mystery'.[94] This seems like over-interpretation.

[91] Jonathan Lear, *Freud* (London: Routledge, 2005), 121.

[92] Ibid. 118.

[93] Letter to Martha Bernays, 8 Nov. 1885, in Freud, *Letters*, 190–3; Decker, *Freud, Dora, and Vienna*, 133–4.

[94] Janet Malcolm, *Psychoanalysis: The Impossible Profession* (London: Pan Books, 1982), 97.

Freud's Methods

In his 'Recommendations to Physicians Practising Psychoanalysis', in 1912, Freud described the analyst's method as follows. He should listen to the patient with evenly suspended attention, without regarding any detail the patient reveals as more important than any other. 'It will be seen that the rule of giving equal notice to everything is the necessary counterpart to the demand made on the patient that he should communicate everything that occurs to him' (SE xii. 112).[95] If Freud did maintain this neutral attitude, he developed it only gradually and with many exceptions. Raymond de Saussure and Joan Rivière, whom he analysed late in his career, both complained that he did too much of the talking.[96] Much earlier, at the period when he analysed Ida Bauer, Freud sometimes told his patients about his theories in the consulting-room, which naturally made them supply material that matched the theories; thus, in October 1900 he told his patient Hermann Swoboda about Fliess's theory of bisexuality.[97] Freud further lays down that the analyst should maintain absolute clinical detachment. One should model oneself on 'the surgeon, who puts aside all his feelings, even his human sympathy, and concentrates his mental forces on the single aim of performing the operation as skilfully as possible' (SE xi. 115). In fact, however, the success of Freud's analyses depended very much on whether Freud liked and was interested in the patient, on whether the patient humbly accepted his pronouncements or tried to argue back, and on whether the patient brought confirmation of his theories.[98]

[95] For a searching critique of this alleged method, see Donald P. Spence, *Narrative Truth and Historical Truth: Meaning and Interpretation in Psychoanalysis* (New York: Norton, 1982), 25.

[96] Their accounts are quoted in Borch-Jacobsen and Shamdasani, *The Freud Files*, 182.

[97] This got Freud into trouble, since Swoboda repeated the theory to Otto Weininger, who used it in his notorious book *Geschlecht und Charakter* (*Sex and Character*, 1903) and was charged by Fliess with plagiarism, using material transmitted by Freud. See Peter Heller, 'A Quarrel over Bisexuality', in Gerald Chapple and Hans H. Schulte (eds.), *The Turn of the Century: German Literature and Art, 1890–1913* (Bonn: Bouvier, 1983), 87–116.

[98] See the appendix, 'Psychoanalysis Interminable: Freud as a Therapist', in Louis Breger, *Freud: Darkness in the Midst of Vision* (New York: Wiley, 2000), 365–73.

Freud's account of Dora confirms the difference between his precepts and his practice. His manner in the sessions was clearly domineering. 'Freud applauds his own persistence; he speaks of using facts against the patient and reports how he overwhelmed Dora with interpretations, pounding away at her argument, until "Dora disputed the facts no longer." '99 Another commentator puts it even more strongly: 'Freud conducted himself in an adversarial manner that sometimes approached the brutal.'100 It was methods like these that enabled Freud for a while to sustain the seduction theory. Although in later accounts he gave the impression that patients reported such experiences of their own volition, it is clear from his writings at the time that he brought this theory to the consulting-room and imposed it on his patients. In 1896 he wrote:

the fact is that these patients never repeat these stories spontaneously, nor do they ever in the course of a treatment suddenly present the physician with the complete recollection of a scene of this kind. One only succeeds in awakening the psychical trace of a precocious sexual event under the most energetic pressure of the analytic procedure, and against an enormous resistance.101

What this 'energetic pressure' might involve emerges from a letter to Fliess written the following year. Freud was analysing a female cousin of Fliess, referred to only as 'G. de B.'. She suffered from eczema around her mouth and from a speech defect as though her mouth were full. Freud thought these ailments went back to her sucking her father's penis as a child, and 'thrust the explanation at her'. G. de B. put up 'the most vehement resistance', whereupon, Freud recounts, 'I have threatened to send her away and in the process convinced myself that she has already gained a good deal of certainty which she is reluctant to acknowledge'.102

It was not only by forcing interpretations on G. de B. and Dora, but also by speaking bluntly about sexual matters, that Freud

---

99 Philip Rieff, *Freud: The Mind of the Moralist*, 3rd edn. (Chicago and London: University of Chicago Press, 1979), quoting SE vii. 104.

100 Mahony, *Freud's Dora*, 14.

101 Freud, 'Heredity and the Aetiology of the Neuroses', SE iii. 153.

102 *Letters of Freud to Fliess*, 220–1 (3 Jan. 1897).

verged on brutality. There is, after all, no neutral way of talking about sexuality, no middle way between the vulgar and the scientific, and the latter was bound to feel like an inappropriate intrusion into a very personal, emotional sphere. Other patients were offended by Freud's bluntness. In *The Interpretation of Dreams* he tells how a female patient's dream involving butcher's meat and unidentifiable vegetables was given a cryptic but evidently sexual interpretation. In a footnote he adds that 'the patient's dream conceals a fantasy of indecent, sexually provocative behaviour on my part, which she repulses'.[103] This may suggest that Freud's interpretation of her dream was felt by the patient as indirect sexual aggression.

How might an analyst have treated Dora differently? Freud's analysis centres on his interpretation of her two dreams. The manifest content must be treated only as clues to the latent content, which the dream-work has rearranged and disguised. Yet Philip McCaffrey's sensitive study of Dora's second dream and of Freud's handling of it has shown that Freud deviates from his own principles by basing part of his interpretation on links which exist only in the manifest content.[104] More strikingly, McCaffrey approaches the dream by treating its manifest content as an aesthetic construction, harmoniously composed and rendered coherent by a pattern of interconnected themes. Thus, the dream falls into three parts, in each of which Dora is removed from the centre of the action: she is in a strange town, unable to find the station, and at home when her family are attending her father's funeral. The three sections are unified by themes of travel, by references to time being translated into space (as when the station is said to be two-and-a-half hours away), and of knowledge: Dora initially does not know that her father was dead, she then does not know the way to the station, but finally she is reading a book which will give her access to knowledge. The themes of travel and time suggest that Dora is on a journey towards independence which requires the death of her father in order to remove an obstacle to her search for knowledge. 'Dora's dream includes a veritable

---

[103] Freud, *The Interpretation of Dreams*, 142.
[104] McCaffrey, *Freud and Dora*, 124–30.

wealth of features which psychoanalytic theory entirely over-looks. The dream is a busy complexity of plot, character, imagery, structure, theme and tone.'[105] It also—one may add—has social implications. Dora was plainly an intelligent young woman who compensated for her inadequate education by attending lectures and by what Freud calls, without further specifying them, serious studies. In her dream the death of the patriarch leaves her free to read a book undisturbed by her family.

Postscript

We now move from case history to history and from 'Dora' back to Ida Bauer. In May 1901 the Zellenkas' daughter died. Ida paid them a visit of condolence, and both admitted their erotic schemes. She reported this to Freud when she called on him in April 1902 to congratulate him on his appointment to a professorship. On that occasion she was suffering from severe facial neuralgia, which Freud interpreted as a psychosomatic self-punishment for having slapped Zellenka in the face. In December 1903 Ida married Ernst Adler, an engineer and composer, nine years her senior (appar-ently not the young engineer whom Freud mentions as a possible suitor).[106] They had a son in 1905. Soon after that, Ida and Ernst converted to Protestantism, presumably to avoid the stigma asso-ciated with Judaism. Her husband, having been unsuccessful as a musician, was taken into her father's business and worked there until the First World War, when he served in the armed forces but returned permanently handicapped with a severe head- and ear-injury affecting his memory and balance. He died in 1932. Meanwhile, Ida became an expert in playing bridge, with Peppina Zellenka as her partner.[107]

In 1923 Ida, temporarily bedridden with Ménière's disease (a disorder of the inner ear that disturbs hearing and balance), received a visit from Dr Felix Deutsch, a follower of Freud's, and complained to him about her unhappy marriage, her husband's

---

[105] Ibid. 38.
[106] The name is supplied by Mahony, *Freud's Dora*, 14.
[107] Decker, *Freud, Dora, and Vienna*, 175–6; Mahony, *Freud's Dora*, 17.

unconcern about her sufferings, and her son's neglect: he had begun to go out in the evenings, she suspected he was interested in girls, and she always stayed awake and listened till he came home.[108] In addition to the continuing vaginal discharges, she now suffered from occasional difficulties in breathing and from coughing-fits in the morning, which she attributed to her excessive smoking. Deutsch worked out that she was none other than 'Dora', and she showed pride in having provided a famous case history.

Many years later, Deutsch, now an émigré in the United States, published an article recounting his meeting with 'Dora' and adding some more recently acquired information about her later life. Her mother had died of cancer in 1912, and her father the following year. Her brother Otto was obliged in 1938 to flee from the Nazis to Paris, where he died of a heart attack. Ida herself managed to emigrate to New York, where she died of cancer in 1945. According to Deutsch's informant, she was an unhappy person. She was obsessed till the end of her life with the state of her bowels—a version of her mother's cleanliness mania. 'Her death from a cancer of the colon, which was diagnosed too late for a successful operation, seemed a blessing to those who were close to her. She had been, as my informant phrased it, "one of the most repulsive hysterics" he had ever met.'[109] More charitably, one may say that Ida Bauer suffered the tragic fate which is implicit in Freud's concept of the Oedipus complex. You have to overcome your father or mother in order to take his or her place in adult life, but the penalty is that you grow into the figure you have displaced. Having spent her youth resisting her mother, Ida grew into a version of her mother.

Ida's three months with Freud, it seems, did not help her. Assuming that the account of her family situation given in the case

[108] Felix Deutsch, 'A Footnote to Freud's "Fragment of an Analysis of a Case of Hysteria"', in Bernheimer and Kahane (eds.), *In Dora's Case*, 35–43; originally published in *Psychoanalytic Quarterly*, 26 (1957), 159–67. Deutsch's account must be read with caution. For example, he says he saw 'Dora' in autumn 1922, whereas other evidence suggests that they met in March 1923: see Mahony, *Freud's Dora*, 16, referring to Paul Roazen, 'Freud's Dora and Felix Deutsch', *Psychologist/Psychoanalyst*, 15 (1994), 34–6.

[109] Deutsch, 'Footnote', 43.

history corresponds even roughly to the truth, it is difficult to see what could have helped her. If it had been possible for her to obtain an education commensurate with her abilities, and thus to distance herself from her family and build up her independence, that would surely have been beneficial. Education and independence, however, were not among her options. Instead, she found herself regularly visiting the consulting-room of an ambitious nerve-specialist who was excited by his innovatory theories and wanted to confirm and extend them. If her illness was in part produced by her situation among men—her father and Hans Zellenka—who wanted to exploit her, the solution reached was to pass her on to another such man, who happened to be the ambitious scientist Freud.

What general conclusion, finally, does this re-examination of Freud's 'Dora' text suggest about psychoanalysis? Freud's methods were wilful, his interpretations fanciful. His other two case histories, those of the Rat Man and the Wolf Man, are no better.[110] We must presume that Freud was often equally arbitrary in the many treatments of which he did not publish an account but from which he drew theoretical conclusions. Yet all generalizations in psychoanalysis, as elsewhere, must be derived from empirical observations. It would seem, then, that the vast edifice of psychoanalysis rests on the flimsiest of foundations, or rather that it floats in the air, like Swift's island of Laputa. Its theoretical assumptions determine its empirical observations, rather than the other way round. It has been pointed out that in the debate between Melanie Klein and Anna Freud and their respective followers that took place in London in the 1940s, 'not a single reference is made to a psychoanalytical fact or observation that might have helped resolve the considerable differences between the two positions'.[111]

Nevertheless, psychoanalysis has not gone away. Although in universities it is more likely to be taught in departments of literature than in departments of psychology, it permeates our common-sense assumptions about human behaviour. Some good

[110] For a memorably trenchant summary of the Wolf Man case, see Porter, *A Social History of Madness*, 223–8.
[111] Macmillan, *Freud Evaluated*, 587.

reasons are easy to find. Not only are Freud's writings beguiling in their construction, style, and rhetoric, but they contain many profound and searching reflections on human nature. Freud is compelling, for example, when he examines why people insist on making themselves unhappy, whether by clinging to the lost object ('Mourning and Melancholia', SE xiv. 243–58) or by getting trapped in the inertia of a painful but familiar routine ('Beyond the Pleasure Principle', SE xviii. 7–64). Such insights remain valid even after the rigid Freudian system that used to surround them has evaporated. Hence Freud remains as much worth reading as the philosopher Schopenhauer, whom he himself read attentively, though only late in life.[112] We no longer read Schopenhauer for his philosophy. His concept of the all-powerful Will is as imaginary as its descendant, the Freudian id. But as a stylist, a moralist, a sceptical commentator on human life, Schopenhauer remains invaluable, as does Freud.

'If you look at everything critically,' remarked the Wolf Man long after his four-year treatment, 'there isn't much in psychoanalysis that will stand up. Yet it helped me.'[113] While many of Freud's patients felt that his treatment had in no way cured them, others found the experience positive.[114] Psychoanalysis, and various associated forms of psychotherapy, have since helped many people. It is a plausible surmise that what has helped them has not been the application of a system but the ability of the analyst or therapist to respond sensitively to the patient and to encourage the patient to feel himself or herself an object of interest. Analysis has recently been described by Michael Brearley, the former cricketer who is now a psychoanalyst, as essentially a relationship between analyst and patient.[115] What goes on within this

---

[112] See Freud's letter of 1 Aug. 1919, in Sigmund Freud and Lou Andreas-Salomé, *Letters*, ed. Ernst Pfeiffer (London: The Hogarth Press, 1972), 99. Earlier references, however, suggest considerable indirect knowledge: see Borch-Jacobsen and Shamdasani, *The Freud Files*, 106; Angus Nicholls and Martin Liebscher (eds.), *Thinking the Unconscious: Nineteenth-Century German Thought* (Cambridge: Cambridge University Press, 2010).

[113] Obholzer, *The Wolf-Man Sixty Years After*, 32.

[114] Breger, *Freud*, 370.

[115] Michael Brearley, 'What Do Psychoanalysts Do?', in Louise Braddock and Michael Lacewing (eds.), *The Academic Face of Psychoanalysis: Papers in Philosophy, the Humanities and the British Clinical Tradition* (London: Routledge, 2007), 20–32.

relationship does not resemble the administration of medication by a doctor; it is more like teaching. Good teaching does not consist in supplying the learner with answers, as Freud evidently did for 'Dora', but in helping the learner to learn. The analyst seeks to guide the patient towards greater self-understanding, and, in particular, towards understanding those aspects of the self which have been screened out, blocked off, or otherwise rejected. Though psychoanalysis has sometimes, as in the case of 'Dora', been disempowering and even damaging, it can also free patients from an artificial misery and restore them, in Freud's famous phrase, to 'common unhappiness'.[116]

[116] SE ii. 305.

NOTE ON THE TEXT

FREUD wrote up his case history of 'Dora' rapidly in January 1901, entitling it 'Dream and Hysteria'. For reasons that cannot now be ascertained, he did not publish it until 1905, when it appeared in the journal *Monatsschrift für Psychiatrie und Neurologie* (*Psychiatric and Neurological Monthly*). It appeared with some additional footnotes in the *Gesammelte Werke* (*Collected Works*) in 1924. Other than that, Freud did not change the text in successive republications.

Footnotes by Freud that simply provide bibliographical information have here been given references to the *Standard Edition of the Complete Psychological Works of Sigmund Freud*, ed. James Strachey, 24 vols. (London: The Hogarth Press, 1953–74), with the abbreviation SE and volume number. References to *The Interpretation of Dreams* are to the translation by Joyce Crick, Oxford World's Classics (Oxford: Oxford University Press, 1999), which is based on the first edition. Asterisks in the text signal an explanatory note at the back of the book.

SELECT BIBLIOGRAPHY

Biography

Appignanesi, Lisa, and John Forrester, *Freud's Women* (London: Weidenfeld & Nicolson, 1992).

Balmary, Marie, *Psychoanalyzing Psychoanalysis: Freud and the Hidden Fault of the Father*, tr. Ned Lukacher (Baltimore: Johns Hopkins University Press, 1982).

Breger, Louis, *Freud: Darkness in the Midst of Vision* (New York: Wiley, 2000).

Clark, Ronald W., *Freud: The Man and the Cause* (London: Weidenfeld & Nicolson, 1980).

Freud, Martin, *Glory Reflected: Sigmund Freud—Man and Father* (London: Angus & Robertson, 1957).

Gay, Peter, *Freud: A Life for our Time* (London: Dent, 1988).

Jones, Ernest, *Sigmund Freud: Life and Work*, 3 vols. (London: The Hogarth Press, 1953–7).

Krüll, Marianne, *Freud and his Father*, tr. Arnold J. Pomerans (London: Hutchinson, 1987).

Roazen, Paul, *Freud and his Followers* (New York: Knopf, 1975).

Roith, Estelle, *The Riddle of Freud: Jewish Influences on his Theory of Female Sexuality* (London and New York: Tavistock Publications, 1987).

General Studies

Borch-Jacobsen, Mikkel, and Sonu Shamdasani, *The Freud Files: An Inquiry into the History of Psychoanalysis* (Cambridge: Cambridge University Press, 2012).

Bowlby, Rachel, *Freudian Mythologies: Greek Tragedies and Modern Identities* (Oxford: Oxford University Press, 2007).

Fisher, Seymour, and Roger P. Greenberg, *The Scientific Credibility of Freud's Theories and Therapy* (New York: Basic Books, 1977).

Grubrich-Simitis, Ilse, *Back to Freud's Texts: Making Silent Documents Speak*, tr. Philip Slotkin (New Haven and London: Yale University Press, 1996), on Freud's manuscripts.

Grünbaum, Adolf, *The Foundations of Psychoanalysis: A Philosophical Critique* (Berkeley, Los Angeles, and London: University of California Press, 1984).

Laplanche, J., and J.-B. Pontalis, *The Language of Psycho-Analysis*, tr. Donald Nicholson-Smith (London: The Hogarth Press, 1973).

Lear, Jonathan, *Love and its Place in Nature: A Philosophical Interpretation of Freudian Psychoanalysis* (London: Faber, 1990).

Macmillan, Malcolm, *Freud Evaluated: The Completed Arc* (Cambridge, Mass.: MIT Press, 1997).

Mitchell, Juliet, *Psychoanalysis and Feminism* (London: Allen Lane, 1974).

Prawer, S. S., *A Cultural Citizen of the World: Sigmund Freud's Knowledge and Use of British and American Writings* (London: MHRA and Maney, 2009).

Rieff, Philip, *Freud: The Mind of the Moralist*, 3rd edn. (Chicago and London: University of Chicago Press, 1979).

Spence, Donald P., *Narrative Truth and Historical Truth: Meaning and Interpretation in Psychoanalysis* (New York: Norton, 1982).

Stevens, Richard, *Freud and Psychoanalysis* (Milton Keynes: Open University Press, 1983), a good introduction.

Webster, Richard, *Why Freud Was Wrong: Sin, Science and Psychoanalysis* (London: HarperCollins, 1995), the most comprehensive negative critique.

Wollheim, Richard, *Freud* (London: Collins, 1971).

The Case of Dora

Bernheimer, Charles, and Claire Kahane (eds.), *In Dora's Case: Freud—Hysteria—Feminism* (New York: Columbia University Press, 1985).

Cixous, Hélène, and Catherine Clément, *The Newly Born Woman*, tr. Betsy Wing (Manchester: Manchester University Press, 1986).

Decker, Hannah S., *Freud, Dora, and Vienna 1900* (New York: Free Press, 1991).

Jacobus, Mary, 'Dora and the Pregnant Madonna', in her *Reading Woman: Essays in Feminist Criticism* (London: Methuen, 1986), 137–93.

Loewenberg, Peter, 'Austro-Marxism and Revolution: Otto Bauer, Freud's "Dora" Case, and the Crises of the First Austrian Republic', in his *Decoding the Past: The Psychohistorical Approach* (New York: Knopf, 1983), 161–204.

McCaffrey, Philip, *Freud and Dora: The Artful Dream* (New Brunswick, NJ: Rutgers University Press, 1984).

Mahony, Patrick J., *Freud's Dora: A Psychoanalytic, Historical, and Textual Study* (New Haven and London: Yale University Press, 1996).

Marcus, Steven, 'Freud and Dora: Story, History, Case History', in his *Representations: Essays on Literature and Society* (New York: Random House, 1976), 247–310.

Sprengnether, Madelon, *The Spectral Mother: Freud, Feminism and Psychoanalysis* (Ithaca and London: Cornell University Press, 1990).

Stadlen, Anthony, 'Was Dora "Ill"?', in Laurence Spurling (ed.), *Sigmund Freud: Critical Assessments*, 4 vols. (London and New York: Routledge, 1989), ii. 196–203.

Hysteria

McGrath, William J., *Freud's Discovery of Psychoanalysis: The Politics of Hysteria* (Ithaca and London: Cornell University Press, 1986).

Micale, Mark S., *Approaching Hysteria: Disease and its Interpretations* (Princeton: Princeton University Press, 1995).

Mitchell, Juliet, *Mad Men and Medusas: Reclaiming Hysteria* (New York: Basic Books, 2000).

Showalter, Elaine, *Hystories: Hysterical Epidemics and Modern Culture* (London: Picador, 1997).

Intellectual and Historical Context

Anderson, Harriet, *Utopian Feminism: Women's Movements in fin-de-siècle Vienna* (New Haven and London: Yale University Press, 1992).

Beller, Steven, *Vienna and the Jews, 1867–1938: A Cultural History* (Cambridge: Cambridge University Press, 1989).

Braddock, Louise, and Michael Lacewing (eds.), *The Academic Face of Psychoanalysis: Papers in Philosophy, the Humanities and the British Clinical Tradition* (London and New York: Routledge, 2007).

Buhle, Mari Jo, *Feminism and its Discontents: A Century of Struggle with Psychoanalysis* (Cambridge, Mass.: Harvard University Press, 1998).

Ellenberger, Henri F., *The Discovery of the Unconscious: The History and Evolution of Dynamic Psychiatry* (1970; London: Fontana, 1994).

Forrester, John, *Language and the Origins of Psychoanalysis* (London: Macmillan, 1980).

Gay, Peter, *Freud, Jews and Other Germans* (New York: Oxford University Press, 1978).

Gresser, Moshe, *Dual Allegiance: Freud as a Modern Jew* (Albany, NY: State University of New York Press, 1994).

Nicholls, Angus, and Martin Liebscher (eds.), *Thinking the Unconscious: Nineteenth-Century German Thought* (Cambridge: Cambridge University Press, 2010).

Ritvo, Lucille B., *Darwin's Influence on Freud* (New Haven and London: Yale University Press, 1990).

Rozenblit, Marsha L., *The Jews of Vienna: Assimilation and Identity* (Albany, NY: State University of New York Press, 1983).

Schaffner, Anna Katharina, *Modernism and Perversion* (Basingstoke: Palgrave Macmillan, 2012).

Schorske, Carl E., *Fin-de-siècle Vienna: Politics and Culture* (Cambridge: Cambridge University Press, 1981).

Sulloway, Frank J., *Freud, Biologist of the Mind: Beyond the Psychoanalytic Legend*, 2nd edn. (Cambridge, Mass., and London: Harvard University Press, 1992).

Wistrich, Robert S., *The Jews of Vienna in the Age of Franz Joseph* (Oxford: Oxford University Press, 1989).

Freud as a Writer

Cohn, Dorrit, 'Freud's Case Histories and the Question of Fictionality', in Joseph H. Smith and Humphrey Morris (eds.), *Telling Facts: History and Narration in Psychoanalysis* (Baltimore and London: Johns Hopkins University Press, 1992), 21–47. (A shortened version in *Oxford German Studies*, 25 (1996), 1–23.)

Frankland, Graham, *Freud's Literary Culture* (Cambridge: Cambridge University Press, 1999).

Hyman, Stanley Edgar, *The Tangled Bank: Darwin, Marx, Frazer and Freud as Imaginative Writers* (New York: Atheneum, 1974).

Mahony, Patrick J., *Freud as a Writer* (New Haven and London: Yale University Press, 1987).

Translating Freud

Bettelheim, Bruno, *Freud and Man's Soul* (London: The Hogarth Press, 1983).

Gilman, Sander L., 'Reading Freud in English: Problems, Paradoxes, and a Solution', in his *Inscribing the Other* (Lincoln, Nebr., and London, 1991), 191–210.

Ornston, Darius Gray (ed.), *Translating Freud* (New Haven and London: Yale University Press, 1992).

Timms, Edward, and Naomi Segal (eds.), *Freud in Exile: Psychoanalysis and its Vicissitudes* (New Haven and London: Yale University Press, 1988).

Further Reading in Oxford World's Classics

Freud, Sigmund, *The Interpretation of Dreams*, trans. Joyce Crick, ed. Ritchie Robertson.

A CHRONOLOGY OF SIGMUND FREUD

1856   6 May: Sigismund (later Sigmund) Freud born at Freiberg (now Příbor) in Moravia.

1860   The Freud family settles in Vienna, after a stay in Leipzig.

1873   Freud enters Vienna University as medical student.

1876–82 Works under Ernst Brücke at the Institute of Physiology in Vienna.

1881   Graduates as Doctor of Medicine.

1882   Becomes engaged to Martha Bernays.

1882–5 Works in Vienna General Hospital, concentrating on cerebral anatomy.

1884   Begins research on the clinical uses of cocaine. July: publishes his paper 'On Cocaine'.

1885   Appointed *Privatdozent* (university lecturer) in neuropathology.

1885   October: begins studies under J. M. Charcot at the Salpêtrière (hospital for nervous diseases) in Paris (until February 1886); becomes interested in hypnosis.

1886   Marries Martha Bernays.

1886–93 Continues work on neurology at the Kassowitz Institute in Vienna.

1887   Birth of eldest child, Mathilde.
       Gets to know the Berlin physician Wilhelm Fliess; their intellectual relationship, intense throughout the 1890s, cools by 1902.

1888   Begins to follow Josef Breuer in using hypnosis for cathartic treatment of hysteria.

1889   Birth of eldest son, Martin.

1891   Birth of second son, Oliver.

1892   Birth of youngest son, Ernst.

1893   Birth of second daughter, Sophie.

1895   Birth of youngest child, Anna (later a distinguished psychoanalyst in her own right).
       Publication with Breuer of *Studies on Hysteria*.

1896 Death of Freud's father Jakob, aged 80.

1897 Freud's self-analysis and 'creative illness', leading to the theory of the Oedipus complex.

Appointment of Gustav Mahler as director of Imperial Opera in Vienna; his informal analysis with Freud took place in 1910.

April: appointment of the anti-Semite Karl Lueger as Mayor of Vienna; only after his fifth electoral victory would the Emperor confirm him in office.

August: First Zionist Congress organized in Basle by Theodor Herzl.

1899 November: publication of *The Interpretation of Dreams*.

1900 October–December: treatment of Ida Bauer ('Dora').

1901 Publication of *The Psychopathology of Everyday Life*.

1902 Appointed Professor Extraordinarius.

1903 Publication of Otto Weininger's notorious *Sex and Character*, which shares with Freud and Fliess a theory of bisexuality.

1905 *Three Essays on the History of Sexuality*.
      Fragment of an Analysis of a Case of Hysteria.

1906 Contact with C. G. Jung, whose adherence to psychoanalysis Freud particularly values; close relationship till their final breach in 1914.

1913 *Totem and Taboo*, in which Freud applies psychoanalysis to explain the origins of culture.

1914 Assassination of heir to the Austrian throne, Archduke Franz Ferdinand, at Sarajevo and outbreak of First World War, in which Austrian troops suffered heavy losses especially on the Russian and Italian fronts.

1915 Freud responds to the War with 'Thoughts for the Times on War and Death'.

1916 21 November: death of Emperor Franz Joseph I of Austria.

1918 Dissolution of Austro-Hungarian Empire; November: proclamation of Austrian Republic.

1920 Death of Freud's daughter Sophie.

1923 *The Ego and the Id*: the conscious/unconscious/preconscious triad of *The Interpretation* is finally replaced with the division of the mind into ego, id, and superego.

1930 *Civilization and its Discontents*, perhaps the greatest of Freud's sociological works.

Awarded the Goethe Prize for his literary and scientific achievement by the City of Frankfurt.

Death of Freud's mother Amalie, aged 95.

1933 After Hitler's seizure of power in Germany, books by Freud are burnt in Berlin.

1938 Hitler's annexation of Austria; Freud leaves Vienna for London.

1939 23 September: death in London.

A CASE OF HYSTERIA

FOREWORD

IF, after an interval of some time, I set to work to substantiate the claims I made in the years 1895 and 1896 about the pathogenesis of hysterical symptoms and the mental processes that occur in hysteria, by describing in full the history of a case and its treatment, I cannot dispense with this foreword, which on the one hand is intended to justify my actions in various respects, and on the other to reduce any expectations of its reception to a reasonable measure.

It was certainly difficult for me to have to publish the results of research—results of such a surprising and unflattering nature—when my professional colleagues were unable to check my assertions. However, it is hardly less difficult for me to begin now by making some of the material from which I derived those results available to the judgement of the general public. I shall not escape blame for that. If it was said at the time that I gave no information about the patients whom I treated, it will be said now that I have given more information on them than is admissible. I hope it will be the same people who now change their reasons for criticizing me like that, and I will say at once that I can never expect to disarm such critics.

Even if I do not spare another thought for those who lack any understanding of me and wish me ill, I always find the publication of my case histories a hard task. The difficulties are partly of a technical nature, arising from the nature of the circumstances. If I am correct in saying that the cause of hysterical disorders is to be found in the intimate details of the patients' psychosexual lives, and their hysterical symptoms express their most secret, repressed desires, casting light on a case of hysteria will inevitably reveal those intimacies and give away those secrets. I am sure that my patients would never have told me anything if the possibility of scientific evaluation of their confessions had crossed their minds, and equally sure that it would be wholly useless to ask the patients themselves for permission to publish. In such circumstances people of delicate sensibilities and probably a timorous disposition would point to a doctor's duty of discretion, and regretfully decline to offer their services to medical science in the cause of enlightenment. However, I think that a doctor has duties not only to his individual patients, but also to scientific knowledge. By duties to scientific knowledge, I mean that the heart of the matter is to serve the many other patients who are suffering or will suffer from the same malady. Then publishing what we think we know about the cause and structure of hysteria becomes a duty, and so long as we can avoid direct personal damage to the individual patient, neglecting it amounts to disgraceful cowardice. I think I have done everything possible to make sure that no such damage is done to the patient discussed here. I have chosen someone whose life was lived not in Vienna, but in a small town a long way off, and whose personal circumstances would therefore be virtually unknown in the capital; I have kept the secret of my treatment of her so carefully from the first that only a single, entirely trustworthy colleague of mine can know that the girl had been my patient. After the end of her treatment I waited another four years before publishing, until I heard of a change in her life allowing me to assume that her own interest in the events and mental processes described here must now have faded. It may be taken for granted that I have given no name that could lead a lay reader to think of her; publication in a strictly scientific medical journal should, moreover, protect the narrative from any such unqualified readers. Of course I cannot avert the possibility of my patient's feeling some pain herself if her own case history happens to fall into her hands. However, she would learn nothing from it that she does not know already, and may ask herself who else can conclude from it that she is the patient discussed.

I know that there are many doctors—in this city, at least—who, regrettably enough, will read such a case history not as a contribution to the psychopathology of neurosis, but as a *roman à clef** intended to amuse them. I can assure such readers that similar guarantees of secrecy will preserve all my case histories still to be written up from their sharp wits, although giving that assurance must limit the use I can make of my material to a very considerable extent.

In this one case history—which I have been able, so far, to extricate from the restrictions of medical discretion and unfavourable circumstances—sexual relationships are discussed frankly, the organs and functions of sexual life are called by their right names, and my account may well give readers with a strong sense of propriety the impression that I did not shrink from discussing such subjects, in such language, with a young woman. Am I supposed to defend myself against that accusation too? I simply claim the rights of the gynaecologist—or rather, very much less than those rights—and say that for anyone to consider conversations of that nature a good means of exciting or satisfying sexual desires is the sign of a perverse and strangely prurient mind. Here I am also inclined to express my opinion in words borrowed from another writer.

'It is pitiful to have to make room for such protestations and assurances in a scientific work, but no one need blame me. Instead, blame the spirit of the times, which leaves us in the happy position where no serious book can now be sure of surviving.'[1]

I will now describe my way of overcoming the technical difficulties of writing an account of this case history. Those difficulties are very considerable for a doctor who has to conduct six to eight such psychotherapeutic treatments a day, and who cannot make notes during his session with an individual patient, because that would arouse the patient's distrust and disrupt his own survey of the material to be recorded. How to record the history of a long treatment for communication to others is a problem that I have not yet solved. In the present case, two circumstances came to my aid: first, the treatment lasted no more than three months, and second, my explanations centred on two dreams—narrated in the middle and at the end of the course of treatment—and I wrote them down verbatim directly after each session, thus giving myself a firm point of reference for the interwoven interpretations and recollections to which they gave rise. I wrote the case history itself only after the conclusion of the course of treatment, from memory,

[1] Richard Schmidt, *Beiträge zur indischer Erotik* [*Essays on Indian Eroticism*], Leipzig 1902. (In his foreword.)

but while my recollection was still fresh and heightened by my interest in publication. The written record is thus not narrated absolutely word for word, but it can claim a high degree of reliability. Nothing of importance was changed, except perhaps for the sequence of explanations in a number of passages, and I did that to show how they connected up.

Let me point out what is to be found in this account and what is missing from it. The work was originally entitled 'Dream and Hysteria', because it seemed to me particularly relevant to showing how the interpretation of dreams weaves itself into the narrative of the treatment, and how, with its help, instances of amnesia can be filled in and symptoms can be explained. In 1900 I had good reason for preceding my intended publications on the psychology of neuroses by a meticulous and deeply penetrating study of dreams,[1] although its reception shows how inadequate an understanding my professional colleagues still had of the subject at that time. In that case, again, there could be no suggestion I had withheld material, so that my ideas would not carry conviction if put to the test, since anyone can subject his own dreams to analytical investigation, and the technique of the interpretation of dreams is easy to learn from the directions and examples that I gave. Today, as then, I must state that immersion in the problems of dreaming is an essential precondition for understanding the psychological processes involved in hysteria and the other psychoneuroses, and that no one who tries to spare himself this preparatory work has any prospect of taking even a few steps in that field. Since this case history presupposes knowledge of the interpretation of dreams, it will be extremely unsatisfactory reading for readers who do not meet that condition. They will be surprised and displeased, rather than finding my explanations satisfactory, and will certainly be inclined to project the cause of their displeasure on the author, whom they will dismiss as a fantasist. In fact, similar displeasure is aroused by the symptoms of the neurosis itself; our medical custom is to obscure such subjects, which will reappear clearly when we try to explain them.

[1] *Die Traumdeutung* [*The Interpretation of Dreams*], Vienna, 1900.

We could avert that reaction only if it were possible to derive the neurosis entirely from factors already known to us. But all probability suggests that, on the contrary, study of the neurosis will induce us to accept many new ideas which will then, gradually, become subjects of definite knowledge. However, novelty has always come up against rejection and resistance.

It would be a mistake to believe that dreams and their interpretation occupy such a prominent position in all psychoanalyses as in this example.

If the present case history seems to give prominence to the exploitation of dreams, in some other respects it is not as full as I could have wished. Its flaws, however, are connected with those very circumstances to which I owe the opportunity of publishing it. I have said above that I would hardly know how to deal with the material for a case history in which treatment went on for, say, a whole year. In this instance, it was possible to survey and recollect incidents occurring over a mere three months, but my findings remain incomplete in more than one respect. The treatment did not go on until it reached the conclusion I had originally envisaged, but was cut short by the patient's own wish when we had reached a certain point. At this time, I had not even tackled several puzzling features of the case yet, and inadequate light had been cast on others, although if I had continued my work on it I would certainly have reached an ultimate conclusion on all points. Here I can therefore offer only a fragment of an analysis.

Perhaps readers familiar with the technique of analysis, as set out in the *Studies in Hysteria*, will be surprised to find that there was no prospect of resolving at least the symptoms being treated within three months. However, that will be understandable when I say that, since the *Studies*, psychoanalytical technique has undergone a complete revolution. At the time, work began by taking the symptoms as a starting-point, and proceeded to a conclusion by resolving them in turn. Since then I have given up that method myself, because I found it entirely inadequate for treating the finer structure of neurosis. I now let patients themselves decide on the subject of each day's work, and we proceed on the basis of the surface phenomena that their unconscious minds bring to their attention. By such means I receive a resolution of symptoms in fragmentary form, with the fragments woven into various contexts over times that may be far apart. In spite of this apparent disadvantage, the new method is far superior to the old, and is undeniably the only one possible.

In view of the fact that my analytical findings in this case were incomplete, there was nothing I could do but emulate those researchers who are lucky enough to unearth invaluable if mutilated remains from antiquity. I have supplemented what was incomplete with the most likely behaviour patterns known to me from other analyses, but like any conscientious archaeologist I have not failed to say, in every case, where my construction follows on from authentic passages.

I have intentionally introduced another kind of incompleteness myself. In general I have not described the work of interpretation that I had to carry out on the ideas and information provided by my patient, only the results. The technique of analytical work is thus, apart from the dreams, revealed only here and there. In this case history I was anxious to show the determination of the symptoms and the intimate construction of the neurotic disorder; if I had also tried to address the other task at the same time it would have led only to hopeless confusion. The material from many case histories would have had to be assembled in order to provide a foundation for the technical and in general empirically determined rules. However, the curtailment involved in omitting to describe technique was not particularly great in this case. The most difficult aspect of technical work did not arise with my patient, since the factor of 'transference' at the end of a case history did not occur in her short course of treatment.

Neither the patient nor the author is responsible for a third way in which this account is incomplete. Rather, it may be taken for granted that a single case history, even if it were complete in itself and no doubt whatever could be cast on it, cannot give the answer to all the questions arising from the problem of hysteria. It cannot teach us to know all varieties of the disorder, all forms of the inner structure of neuroses, all the possible kinds of connection between the psychological and the somatic in hysteria. We may

not justifiably ask any more of a single case than it can provide.
Furthermore, those who have not yet been willing to believe in the
general and exclusive validity of the psychosexual aetiology of
hysteria, will hardly be convinced of it by reading a single case
history, but at best will postpone judgement until they have won
the right to conviction by work of their own.[1]

---

[1] (Added in 1923): The treatment described here was broken off on 31 December
1899 [in fact: 1900], and my account of it written down over the next two weeks, but not
published until 1905. It is not to be expected that over two decades of further work
would not have changed the concept and presentation of such a case, but it would obviously be pointless to bring this case history up to date and adjust it to the present state of
knowledge by making corrections and expanding on the material. I have therefore, in
essence, left it as it was, and merely improved cursory and imprecise expressions drawn
to my attention by my excellent English translators, Mr and Mrs James Strachey. I have
accommodated what I felt were permissible as critical additions in passages such as this,
added to the case history, so that if readers find nothing to the contrary in the added passages, they are justified in concluding that I am still of the same mind today. The problem of medical discretion that concerns me in this foreword is not relevant to the other
case histories in this volume [as originally printed in volume 8 of Freud's *Gesammelte
Schriften*], for three of them were published with the express consent of the patient, or in
the case of little Hans of his father, and in one case (Schreber) the subject of analysis was
not really the man himself but an autobiographical book that he had written. In the case
of Dora, the secret has been kept until this year. I recently heard that my former patient,
who had long disappeared from my knowledge and had just fallen ill of another malady,
has told her doctor that as a girl she was a subject of my analysis, and the information
made it easy for my knowledgeable colleague to identify her as the Dora in the 1899 [cor-
rectly: 1900] case. No thinking person will blame analytical therapy for the fact that the
three months of her treatment did no more than to resolve her conflict at the time, so that
they could not provide protection against later illness.

I

THE CLINICAL PICTURE

I SHOWED in my book *The Interpretation of Dreams*, published in 1900, that dreams in general can be interpreted, and that once the work of interpretation is completed they can be replaced by clearly formed ideas that fit intellectually into a certain connection. In the following pages I would now like to give an example of the only practical use that the art of interpreting dreams seems to allow. In my book[1] I mentioned the way in which I came to the problems of dreams. I came upon it while I was trying to cure psychoneuroses by a particular process of psychotherapy, during which my patients told me, among other incidents in the life of their minds, about dreams that seemed to require to be placed somewhere in the long-drawn-out connection between symptoms of illness and pathogenic ideas. I discovered at the time how, without further instruction, we must translate the language of dreams into a means of expression comprehensible in the terms we normally use to express thoughts. This knowledge, I may say, is essential for a psychoanalyst, for dreaming is one of the ways whereby psychical material can reach the conscious mind although, because its content puts up lively resistance, it has been barred from consciousness, repressed, and thus has become pathogenic. Dreaming, in short, is one of the devices we employ to circumvent repression, one of the main methods of what may be called indirect representation in the mind. The present fragment from the case history of the treatment of a girl with hysteria is intended to show how the interpretation of dreams comes into the work of analysis. At the same time, it offers me an occasion to present some of my views on the psychological processes and organic conditions leading to hysteria for the first time, and broadly enough to preclude any misunderstanding. I hope I need not apologize for that breadth, since it

[1] [See *The Interpretation of Dreams*, tr. Joyce Crick, Oxford World's Classics (Oxford: Oxford University Press, 1999), 80.]

will be admitted that only the most dedicated immersion in the
subject of hysteria allows us to appreciate the great demands it
makes on a doctor and researcher; affecting to dismiss them will
not do. Indeed:

> Not art and science on their own
> But patience also must be shown!*

To offer a complete, fully rounded case history from the start
would amount to providing the reader with conditions very different from those of the medical observer. What the relatives of the
patient—in this case the father of the eighteen-year-old girl—
say usually gives an unrecognizable picture of the course of the
illness. I certainly begin treatment by asking to hear all about
the patient's life and the case itself, but what I hear is still not
enough for me to get my bearings properly. That first narrative
may be compared to an unnavigable river with its bed sometimes
obstructed by rocks, sometimes divided into shallows by sand-
banks. I can only wonder how the smooth, precise case histories of
hysterics given by some authors have come into being. In reality,
patients are unable to give such an account of themselves. They
can certainly provide the doctor with an adequate and coherent
account of this or that period in their lives, but then comes another
period in which what they can say does not go deep, leaving gaps
and riddles behind, and then one keeps coming upon yet other
periods that are entirely in the dark, unilluminated by any useful
account of them. Even the superficial connections are usually
disjointed, the sequence of various events uncertain; during the
narrative the patient herself keeps correcting a fact or a date, and
then, after long indecision, may fall back on what she first said.
A patient's inability to present the story of her life in the proper
order, so far as it coincides with the case history, is not only characteristic of neurosis,[1] it also has great theoretical importance.

---

[1] A colleague of mine once asked me to provide psychotherapeutic treatment for his
sister who, he said, had been treated for hysteria (with pain and impeded mobility) for
years without success. This brief account of her condition seemed perfectly compatible
with the diagnosis; in the first session, I asked my patient to tell me her own story. When
that story turned out to be perfectly clear and consecutive, despite the curious facts to
which it alluded, I told myself that this could not be a case of hysteria, and I immediately

The following factors account for this drawback: first, in her narrative the patient deliberately withholds part of something that is well known to her and that she knows should be included, because she has not yet overcome feelings of timidity and shame (which make her discreet where other persons are involved); this is the consciously dishonest aspect of her account. Secondly, part of the anamnestic knowledge otherwise available to the patient is missed out of her narrative, although she has no reason to withhold it; this is the unconsciously dishonest aspect. Thirdly, there is never any lack of genuine instances of amnesia, gaps in the memory through which not only old but even very recent memories have fallen, and of illusory memories with the secondary function of filling those gaps.[1] Where the facts themselves are preserved in the memory, the intention lying behind instances of amnesia will certainly be revealed by the removal of a connection, and the connection will equally certainly be broken if the sequence of events is changed. That sequence always proves to be the most vulnerable part of our store of memories, and is most often subject to repression. Many memories are, so to speak, in the first stage of repression; typically, the patient has doubts of them. A certain time later, such doubts are replaced by forgetfulness or false memories.[2]

Such a state of the memories relating to the case history is the necessary, *theoretically requisite correlation* of the symptoms of the illness. In the course of treatment, patients supply what they held back or what did not occur to them, although they always knew it. The illusory memories prove to be untenable, the gaps in memory are filled in. If the practical aim of treatment is to remove all possible symptoms and replace them by conscious thoughts, then we

carried out a careful physical examination. As a result, I was able to make a diagnosis of a moderately advanced case of the degenerative disease *tabes*,* which responded to a course of H_g injections (Ol. Cinereum, administered by Professor Lang), and her condition improved considerably.

[1] Instances of amnesia and of illusory memory complement each other. Where there are large gaps in the memory, we find few illusory memories. Conversely, at first sight the latter can entirely obscure the presence of amnesia.

[2] A rule drawn from experience shows that in the case of a memory doubtfully presented, we can disregard that version of the narrator's account. If an account wavers between two forms, we may take the first to be given as the reality, the second as caused by repression.

can consider that another, theoretical aim is to cure all damage to the patient's memory. The two aims coincide: once one is achieved, so is the other, because the same way leads to both.

In the nature of things, as they form the material for psycho-analysis, it follows that in our case histories we ought to pay as much attention to the purely human and social circumstances of patients as to the somatic data and the symptoms of their illness. Above all, our interest will turn to the patient's family circum-stances, and as readers will see, not just to hereditary factors but in other respects as well.

The family circle of my eighteen-year-old patient comprised, besides the girl herself, her parents and a brother who was a year and a half her senior. The dominant figure was the father, both because of his intelligence and his qualities of character, and because of the circumstances of his life, which provide the context for the story of the patient's childhood and her illness. At the time when I began treating the girl, he was a man in the second half of his forties, of more than average enterprise and talent, an industri-alist in a very comfortable financial situation. His daughter felt particular affection for him, and her critical faculty, which devel-oped early, was all the more upset by many of his actions and characteristics.

This affection was also heightened by the many severe maladies to which the father had been subject since she was six. At this time he contracted tuberculosis, and for that reason the family moved to a small town with a pleasant climate in our southern provinces; the lung infection quickly improved there, but since it was thought necessary for him not to overexert himself, the town, which I will call B., was the main place of residence for the family, parents and children alike, for about the next ten years. When the father was in good health he was sometimes away visiting his factories, and in summer they went to a spa resort in the mountains.

When the girl was about ten years old, a detached retina in one eye made it necessary for her father to undergo treatment in a darkened room. This disorder permanently affected his sight. His most serious malady occurred some two years later, and consisted of an attack of confusion associated with symptoms of paralysis and slight psychological disturbances. At the time, a friend of the sick man, whose role in the girl's story will concern us later, persuaded him, since he had improved only slightly, to go to Vienna with his doctor and ask my advice. I hesitated for a while, wondering whether I should not assume that he was suffering from tabo-paresis,* but then decided on a diagnosis of diffuse vascular infection, and after he had admitted to a specific infection before his marriage, I prescribed a course of vigorous anti-syphilitic treatment. As a result, all the symptoms still present disappeared. No doubt I owed it to this happy outcome that four years later the father introduced me to his daughter, who had now clearly become neurotic, and after another two years put her in my hands for psychotherapy.

Meanwhile, I had met a slightly older sister of the father, in whom a severe form of psychoneurosis was present, although without any of the characteristic hysterical symptoms. This woman died, after a life of unhappy marriage, suffering the symptoms, never really fully explained, of a form of rapidly progressing malnutrition.

The father's elder brother, whom I occasionally met, was a bachelor and a hypochondriac.

The girl who became my patient at the age of eighteen had always liked her father's side of the family best, and after she fell ill regarded the aunt mentioned above as her model. I had no doubt that she took after his family in her talents and her precocious intellectual development, as well as her poor health. I did not meet her mother. Judging by what both father and daughter said, I formed the impression that she was not very highly educated, and above all not very clever, and that especially following her husband's illness and the subsequent rift between them she concentrated entirely on looking after the household, appearing to be an example of what we could call 'housewife psychosis'. She was remote from her children's more active interests, and filled her days with cleaning the apartment, its furnishings, and the household appliances and keeping them all spotless, to an extent that made it almost impossible for her simply to use and enjoy her home surroundings. Inevitably one classifies this state of mind—and plenty of normal housewives show signs of it—with compulsive hand-washing and similar obsessions with cleanliness, but in such normal women, and in our patient's mother, there is no understanding that they are sick, which is an essential feature of compulsive neurosis. The relationship between mother and daughter had been very cool for years. The daughter ignored her mother, criticized her harshly, and had withdrawn from her influence entirely.[1]

The girl's only brother, who was a year and a half older than she was, had been her model in earlier years, and her ambition made her try to emulate him. The relationship between the two siblings had not been so close in recent years. The young man tried to extricate himself as far as possible from the complexities of his family's life; when he had to take sides, he supported his mother. So the usual sexual attraction brought father and daughter closer together on one side of the family, mother and son on the other.

Our patient, whom I shall call Dora from now on, was already showing nervous symptoms when she was eight years old. At this time she began suffering from permanent and sometimes very marked breathlessness, which first set in after a little climbing expedition, and so was thought to be the result of overexertion. In the course of six months her condition slowly improved under the rest treatment prescribed for her. The family doctor seems never

---

[1] I do not consider that heredity is the only cause of hysteria, but particularly with reference to earlier publications ('L'Hérédité et l'étiologie des névroses', *Revue neurologique*, 1896 ['Heredity and the Aetiology of the Neuroses', SE iii. 141–56]), in which I oppose the proposition above, I would not wish to give the impression of underestimating heredity in the aetiology of hysteria, or of thinking that the idea can be dispensed with altogether. In our patient's case, sufficient factors to induce illness were present in what I have said about her father and his siblings; indeed, anyone who is of the opinion that even cases of a disorder like the mother's are impossible without a hereditary disposition to it will be able to explain heredity in this case as a convergent factor. But another one seems to me more significant in the girl's hereditary or rather constitutional disposition. I have mentioned that before his marriage her father had contracted syphilis. A *strikingly large* percentage of the patients I have treated by psychoanalysis are the offspring of fathers who have suffered from *tabes* or paralysis. In the recent conference on the descendants of syphilitics (XIIIth International Congress on Medicine in Paris, 2–9 August 1900, in papers delivered by Finger, Tarnowky, Jullien, etc.) I find no mention of the fact that my own experience as a neuropathologist forces me to recognize: a father's syphilis can easily be regarded as the cause of his children's neuropathological constitution.

to have doubted his diagnosis of a purely nervous disorder, excluding any organic cause of her dyspnoea,* but he obviously thought such a diagnosis could be reconciled with the aetiology of overexertion.[1]

The little girl suffered the usual infectious childhood diseases without any lasting ill-effects. As she told me (intending it to be taken as symbolic!), it was usually her brother who first contracted an illness, and had it only to a minor degree, whereas she then suffered it severely. When she was around twelve, she began to suffer migraine-like headaches on one side of her head, with attacks of nervous coughing, at first always occurring together, until the two symptoms separated and developed in different ways. The migraine came less frequently, and not at all after she was sixteen. The attacks of *tussis nervosa*, probably set off by bad catarrh, went on all the time. When she came to me at the age of eighteen for treatment, she had recently begun coughing in a characteristic way. The number of these attacks could not be established; they lasted for three to five weeks, and once even for several months. In the first half of such an attack, at least in the last few years, her most troublesome symptom had been complete loss of voice. The diagnosis, yet again, that the attacks were caused by nervous strain had been made long before; the many customary treatments tried, including hydrotherapy and localized electric-shock therapy, were unsuccessful. The child, who had grown up in these circumstances to become a mature girl exercising her own independent judgement, used to mock the efforts of the doctors and finally rejected medical assistance. Although she did not dislike the family doctor personally, she had always resisted having him called in to give advice. Any suggestion of consulting another doctor met with opposition from her, and only her father's express command brought her to me.

I first saw her in the early summer of her sixteenth year, when she was suffering coughing and hoarseness, and even then I suggested psychological treatment, an idea that came to nothing when that long attack stopped of its own accord. In the winter of the

---

[1] On the probable cause of this first illness see below.

next year, she was in Vienna after the death of her much-loved aunt, staying with her uncle and his daughters, and while there she suffered a feverish illness diagnosed at the time as appendicitis.[1] In the following autumn, the family finally left the spa resort of B., since her father's state of health seemed to allow it, went to live first in the town where her father had his factory, and scarcely a year later took up permanent residence in Vienna.

By now Dora was a girl in the bloom of youth, with intelligent and pleasing features, but she caused her parents great anxiety. The main signs of her disorder were now low spirits and a change in her character. She was clearly not happy with herself or those close to her, she was unfriendly to her father, and did not get on at all with her mother, who wanted her to help with the work about the house. She tried to avoid company; as far as the weariness and absent-mindedness of which she complained allowed, she occupied herself in attending lectures for ladies and pursuing serious studies. One day her parents were alarmed by a letter that they found on or in the girl's desk, in which she took her leave of them, saying she couldn't bear her life any more.[2] However, her father did not lack insight, and that made him assume that the girl was not seriously proposing to kill herself. He was badly shaken, all the same, and when one day, after a minor altercation with her father, the daughter suffered her first fainting fit,[3] which involved amnesia, it was decided, in spite of her resistance, that she should begin treatment with me.

The case history as I have sketched it out so far hardly seems, on the whole, worth recording. A case of *petite hystérie*, with the usual somatic and psychological symptoms: dyspnoea, *tussis nervosa*,

---

[1] See on this illness the analysis of the second dream.

[2] As I have said above, this cure, and thus my insight into the chain of circumstances involved in the case history, remain fragmentary. I can therefore draw no conclusions on many points, or even evaluate indications and assumptions. When we discussed this letter in one session, the girl asked, as if surprised, 'How could they have found the letter? It was locked in my desk.' But as she knew that her parents had read this draft of a farewell letter, I conclude that she herself made sure it fell into their hands.

[3] I believe that spasms and delirium were also observed in this fit, but as the analysis did not get as far as this event, I can report no certain recollection of the fact.

aphonia or voice-loss, and perhaps she still suffered migraines, along with bad temper, quarrelsome and hysterical outbursts, and professions of *taedium vitae* which were probably not meant seriously. More interesting case histories of hysterics have certainly been published, and have very often been received with more careful attention, but there will be no accounts here of stigmatic marks on sensitive areas of the skin, restricted vision, and similar phenomena. I will allow myself only to comment that none of the collections of strange and remarkable phenomena in hysteria have brought us much further in the understanding of this still mysterious disorder. What we need is enlightenment on precisely the most ordinary cases and their most frequent and typical symptoms. I would have been pleased if circumstances had allowed me to provide a full explanation of this case of *petite hystérie*. From my experience with other patients, I do not doubt that my analytical methods would have enabled me to do so.

In the year 1896, shortly after the publication of my *Studies on Hysteria* in collaboration with Dr J. Breuer, I asked a colleague, a man outstanding in our field, for his opinion of the psychological theory of hysteria proposed in that work. He said frankly that he thought it an unjustified generalization drawn from conclusions that may, in a few cases, be correct. Since then I have seen many cases of hysteria, I have spent days, weeks, or years on each case, and in none of them have I found that those psychological conditions postulated in the *Studies* were absent: psychological trauma, a conflict of affects, and, as I have added in later publications, their effect on a patient's sexual behaviour. In matters that become pathogenic because patients are trying to hide them, it cannot, of course, be expected that those patients will reveal them to the doctor, nor can we give up at the first negative reply to a request for further investigation.[1]

---

[1] Here is an example of the latter. One of my Viennese colleagues, whose conviction that sexual factors were of no importance in hysteria is probably very firmly entrenched, made up his mind to ask a fourteen-year-old girl suffering from alarming hysterical vomiting the delicate question of whether she had ever had any physical experience of love. The child said no, probably with well-assumed astonishment, and told her mother, in her disrespectful way: imagine, that silly man even asked me if I'm in love. I then treated her, and she then revealed—although not at our first discussion—that she had been

With my patient Dora, I owed it to her father's intelligence, which I have already mentioned more than once, that I did not have to search for the connection of her illness with real life, at least in its final form. He told me that he and his family had become close friends in B. with another couple who had lived there for several years. Frau K. had nursed him through his severe illness, which gave her an abiding claim on his gratitude. Herr K., he told me, had always been very kind to his daughter Dora, going for walks with her when he was in B. and giving her little presents, but no one would have seen anything wrong in that. Dora, I also heard, had looked after the couple's two small children with loving care and was almost like a mother to them. When father and daughter visited me in the summer two years ago, they were just leaving to visit Herr and Frau K., who were staying for the summer beside one of our Alpine lakes. Dora was to stay in the K. household for several weeks, while her father planned to travel home a few days later. Herr K. was also present at the time. When her father was preparing for his journey home, however, the girl suddenly said, very firmly, that she wanted to go back with him, and she got her way. Only a few days later did she explain the reason for her unusual conduct, by telling her mother— indicating that the story was to be passed on to her father—that Herr K. had made advances to her on a walk after an outing on the lake. Next time they met her father and uncle asked Herr K., thus accused, to account for himself, whereupon he emphatically denied that he had made any advances deserving such an interpretation and began casting aspersions on the girl, who according to Frau K. showed an interest in sexual matters and nothing else, and had even been reading Mantegazza's *Physiology of Love** and similar books in their lakeside house. Probably, he said, her mind

masturbating for many years, with a strong flux of *fluor albus** (which was clearly linked to her vomiting), and she had finally weaned herself off the practice, but now that she abstained from it she was tormented by violent guilt-feelings, ascribing any accidents that happened in the family to divine punishment for her sin. She was also influenced by the story of her aunt, whose extramarital pregnancy (here was a second determining link with the vomiting) had allegedly been successfully concealed from her. She was regarded as very much a child, but proved to have been initiated into all the essential facts of sexual relationships.

had become overheated by her reading, and the whole incident as she described it was 'imaginary'.

'I have no doubt', said her father, 'that this incident is to blame for Dora's low spirits, irritability, and ideas of suicide. She wants me to break off our contact with Herr K., and particularly with Frau K., whom she used to positively revere. However, I can't do that; first, I myself think Dora's story of the husband's immoral conduct is a fantasy that has taken root in her mind, and secondly feelings of genuine friendship bind me to Frau K., and I would not like to hurt her. Poor woman, she is very unhappy with her husband, of whom, incidentally, I don't have the highest opinion; she has suffered from her nerves a great deal herself, and has found me her only true friend. I am sure that in my state of health I need not assure you that there is nothing wrong in our relationship. We are two unfortunates who console one another as best we may with our friendly sympathy. You know that there is nothing between me and my wife now. Dora, however, who gets her obstinacy from me, cannot be persuaded to overcome her dislike for the Ks. Her last attack was after a conversation in which she repeated her demand to me. Please try to bring her round to a better way of thinking.'

It was not entirely in tune with these revelations that at other times Dora's father tried to lay most of the blame for his daughter's impossible conduct on her mother, whose character made the house uncomfortable for everyone. However, I had already made up my mind not to judge the real facts until I had heard the other side of the story as well.

In Dora's case, her experience with Herr K.—the advances he made to her and the subsequent insult to her honour—would have given rise to the psychological trauma that in the past Breuer and I had postulated as an essential condition for the development of hysterical illness. This new case, however, also illustrates all the difficulties that have since caused me to go beyond that theory,[1]

---

[1] I have gone beyond that theory without giving it up; that is to say, I would now call it incomplete rather than wrong. I have merely given up emphasizing the so-called hypnoid state brought about in the patient by the trauma, which is supposed to serve as the

increased by another and particular kind of difficulty. For the trauma of a life-story that we know is not—and this is a frequent feature in case histories of hysteria—able to explain and determine the unique nature of the symptoms; we would understand just as much or just as little of their connection if symptoms other than *tussis nervosa*, aphonia, low spirits, and a sense of *taedium vitae* had resulted from the trauma. But now comes the added complication that the patient had shown some of these symptoms—the cough, the loss of voice—years before the trauma, and the first manifestations definitely belonged to her childhood, since they occurred in her eighth year of life. If we do not want to abandon traumatic theory, therefore, we must go back to her childhood in search of influences or impressions that can act like a trauma, and it is really remarkable that when we do that, the investigation even of cases where the first symptoms did not set in during childhood has led me to follow the patient's life back to those early years.[1]

After the first difficulties of her treatment had been overcome, Dora told me about an earlier experience with Herr K. that was even more likely to have the effect of a sexual trauma. She was fourteen years old at the time. Herr K. had arranged with her and his wife that the ladies would come to his shop in the main square of B. that afternoon, to watch a church festivity. However, he persuaded his wife to stay at home, told his assistant that she could take time off, and was alone when the girl arrived at the shop. When the church procession was about to begin, he asked her to wait for him at the door to the stairs leading to the floor above, while he let down the roller blinds. He then rejoined her, and instead of going through the open door he suddenly held the girl close and pressed a kiss on her lips. That was exactly the situation likely to give a virginal girl of fourteen a clear sensation of sexual arousal. However, at that moment Dora was overcome by violent

reason for further psychologically abnormal developments. If it is permissible, in a joint work, to make a retrospective division of property, I would like to say here that the establishment of the 'hypnoid state', in which many experts claimed to see the core of our work, sprang exclusively from Breuer. I consider it superfluous and misleading to interrupt the continuity of the problem in which the psychic procedure consists of the formation of hysterical symptoms by giving it that name.

[1] See my treatise 'The Aetiology of Hysteria'. [In SE iii. 191–221.]

revulsion; she tore herself away, hurried past the man to the stairs, and from there to the door of the building. All the same, she did not break off all contact with Herr K.; neither of them ever mentioned this little scene, and she said she had kept the secret to herself until she confessed it in the course of treatment. Immediately after it, she did avoid being alone with Herr K. At the time he and his wife had arranged to go away on an excursion lasting several days, and Dora was to go with them. After that kiss in the shop, she told them she would not be one of their party, without giving any reason.

In this, the second scene to have come to my knowledge although it was chronologically the first, the fourteen-year-old child's conduct is already entirely and fully hysterical. I would without another thought consider anyone a hysteric if a cause for sexual arousal evokes overwhelmingly or exclusively feelings of disgust in her, whether or not she shows somatic symptoms. Casting light on this *affective reversal* remains one of the most important and at the same time difficult tasks in the psychology of neurosis. My own opinion is that I am still some way from that aim; however, in the context of this account I shall be able to describe only a part of what I do know.

The case of our patient Dora is not adequately explained by dwelling on the affective reversal; we must also say that there was a *displacement* of her feelings. Instead of the genital sensation that would certainly have been felt by a healthy girl in such circumstances,[1] she feels disgust associated with the mucous membrane at the entrance to the digestive tract. Lip-contact certainly influenced this localization by means of the kiss, but I also think I detect the influence of another factor.[2]

Dora's disgust at the time did not remain a constant symptom, and at the time of her treatment was only, so to speak, potential. She was eating poorly, and admitted to feeling a slight aversion

---

[1] Assessment of the circumstances will be easier in the light of a later explanation.

[2] The disgust that Dora felt at this kiss cannot have been the result of accidental causes, which she would certainly have remembered and mentioned. I happen to have met Herr K., since it was he who came to see me with the patient's father, and he was a still youthful man of attractive appearance.

to food. On the other hand, the scene with Herr K. also had another consequence: a hallucinatory sensation, that reappeared now and then even when she was talking to me. She said she could still feel the pressure of his embrace on her upper body. I made the following reconstruction of what actually happened in the scene, according to certain rules in the formation of symptoms of which I had become aware, together with further and otherwise inexplicable peculiarities of the patient's conduct; for instance, she did not like to pass a man whom she saw engaged in animated or amicable conversation with a lady. I think that in that stormy embrace she felt not only the kiss on her lips, but also Herr K.'s erect penis pressing against her body. This perception, which disgusted her, was removed from her memory, repressed, and replaced by the harmless sensation of pressure on her thorax, deriving heightened intensity from the real but repressed source. It was, therefore, another displacement from her lower body to her upper body.[1] The compulsive element in her behaviour, however, is formed as if it proceeded from her original memory. She does not like to pass a man who, she thinks, is in a state of sexual arousal, because she does not want to see the somatic sign of it again.

Here, remarkably, three symptoms—disgust, the sensation of pressure on her upper body, and her fear of men engaged in amicable conversation—proceed from a single incident, and we may also note that only relating the three signs of her state of mind to each other makes it possible to understand the formation of the symptoms. Disgust corresponds to the repression of the erogenous zone of the lips (an area made suspect, as we shall discover, by suckling in infancy). The pressure of the erect penis probably resulted in an analogous change in the corresponding female organ, the clitoris, and the arousal of this second erogenous zone was displaced and fixated on the simultaneous sensation of

[1] Such displacements are not assumed for the purposes of this one explanation, but prove to be the requisite of a wide range of symptoms. I later saw the same terror brought about by an embrace (without a kiss) in a fiancée who had been very much in love, and sought my advice because she had suddenly, when she was in low spirits, cooled towards the man to whom she was engaged. Here it was easy to trace her terror back to the man's erection, which she had felt but had then excluded from her conscious mind.

pressure on the thorax. The fear of men in what could be a state of sexual arousal acted like a phobia, securing itself from a revival of the repressed perception.

To explore this possibility further, I very carefully asked the patient whether she knew anything about the physical signs of arousal in the male body. She said yes, now, but at that time she thought not. I took the greatest care with this patient from the first, for fear of giving her new insights into the field of sexual behaviour, not for reasons of conscience but because I wanted to test my assumptions in her case stringently. I therefore called something by its name only when her very clear allusions made a direct reference to it seem a very minor risk to take. She regularly gave prompt and honest answers, saying that yes, she already knew that, but her memories did not solve the puzzle of *how* she knew it. She had forgotten the origin of what she knew.[1]

If I imagine the scene in the shop as I described it, I arrive at this reason for her disgust.[2] The sensation of disgust seems to be originally a reaction to the smell (and later the sight) of excrement. However, the genitals, in particular the penis as the organ that serves to empty the bladder of urine as well as having a sexual function, can suggest the excremental function. Indeed, this function is the first, and before sexual maturity the only, one known to a child. So disgust becomes one of the affective expressions in sexual life. This is the *inter urinas et faeces nascimur** of the Church Father, an idea that clings to sexual activity and cannot be separated from it in defiance of all attempts at idealization. However, let me point out that, as I see it, I do not consider that the problem is solved by tracing that associative path. While such an association *can* be aroused, that does not mean that it *will* be aroused. In normal circumstances it will not. Knowing associative paths does not make it superfluous to know the powers that follow those paths.[3]

*

[1] See the second dream.

[2] Here and in all similar passages we should not be prepared for complex rather than simple reasons, in fact for *over-determination*.

[3] There is much in these remarks that is typical and generally valid in the context of hysteria. The idea of an erection arouses one of the most interesting of hysterical symptoms. A woman's attention, drawn to the outline of the male genitals perceptible under a

Furthermore, it was not easy for me to get my patient to think about her encounters with Herr K. She claimed to have broken with him entirely. The upper level of all her ideas in our sessions, everything that easily came into her mind and that she remembered had been there the day before, always related to her father. It was true that she could not forgive her father for remaining on friendly terms with Herr K., and particularly with Frau K., but her concept of this relationship was not the one that he himself would have wished to be entertained. Dora was in no doubt that an ordinary love-affair linked her father to that beautiful young woman. Nothing that could substantiate this idea had escaped her mercilessly sharp observation, *there were no gaps in her memory on this point.* Her father's acquaintanceship with Herr and Frau K. had begun before his severe illness; however, it became really close only when, during that illness, the young woman positively set herself up as his nurse, while Dora's mother kept away from the sick man's bedside. In the first summer holiday after his recovery there were incidents bound to open everyone's eyes to the true nature of their 'friendship'. The two families had booked a suite in the hotel together, and one day Frau K. said she could not go on sleeping in the bedroom that she had shared so far with one of her children. A few days later her father gave up his own bedroom, and both moved into new rooms, the rooms at the far end of the suite, separated from each other only by the corridor, The rooms they had given up offered no such guarantee against being disturbed. When Dora complained to her father later about Frau K., he used to say he didn't understand her hostility, when his children had every reason to be grateful to her. Dora's Mama, to whom she turned asking for an explanation of this mysterious remark, told her that at that time Papa had been so unhappy that he had meant to commit suicide in the forest. But Frau K., guessing his intentions, had followed him, pleaded with him, and made him decide to stay alive for his family's sake. Of course, said Dora,

man's clothing and then repressed, thus becomes a factor in many cases of shyness and social anxiety. The broad connection between the sexual and the excremental, the pathogenic significance of which can hardly be overestimated, serves as the basis for a great number of hysterical phobias.

she didn't believe that story, the two of them had probably been seen together in the forest, so Papa had made up the suicide story as a pretext for his rendezvous.[1] On their return to B., Papa visited Frau K. every day at certain times when her husband was at his shop. Everyone was talking about it, said Dora, and asking her meaningful questions. Herr K. himself had often complained to her Mama, but spared Dora herself allusions to the subject, which she seemed to ascribe to his delicacy of feeling. When they went for walks together, Papa and Frau K. always managed things so that the two of them were on their own. There was no doubt that she was accepting money from him, because she was spending on things that could not possibly have been covered out of her own means or her husband's. Dora's Papa also began making large presents to her, and in order to cover up for that he also gave particularly generous gifts to Dora's mother and Dora herself. Until then Frau K. had been sickly, and even had to spend some months being treated for her nerves in a clinic because of difficulties with walking, but she was better now and full of life.

Even after they had left B., said Dora, contact between the families continued for several years, while her father said from time to time that the poor climate where they were now living did not suit him, he really must do something to help himself. Then he began coughing and complaining, until he suddenly went off to B. and wrote the most cheerful of letters home. All these disorders were just excuses to go and see his lover again. Then Dora learned one day that her family was moving to Vienna, and she began to suspect some connection. Sure enough, they had hardly been in Vienna for three weeks when she heard that the Ks. had also moved to that city. Indeed, they were there at present, and she often met Papa with Frau K. in the street. She also met Herr K. quite often, he always watched her as she walked on, and one day when he met her on her own he had followed her for some way to find out where she was going and whether she, too, had a rendezvous.

I heard such criticisms of her father as that he was dishonest, there was a touch of falsity in his character, he thought only of his

---

[1] This was with reference to her own show of wishing to commit suicide, which may express her longing for a similar love.

own satisfaction, and had a gift for arranging matters as they suited him best, particularly on those days when he felt that his state of health was declining again, and went away to B. for several weeks, whereupon the perceptive Dora had soon found out that Frau K. too was on a trip to the same place to visit her relations.

I could not find fault with Dora's account of her father's character in general, and it was also easy to see in which particular accusation she was right. When she was in an embittered mood, the idea that she had been delivered up to Herr K.'s mercies as a price for his toleration of the relationship between Dora's father and his wife came forcibly into her mind, and one could guess at her anger with her father, concealed behind her love for him, for making use of her in such a way. At other times she knew that she would have been guilty of exaggeration in saying such things. Of course, the two men never concluded a formal agreement in which she was an object of barter; her father in particular would have shrunk in horror from such an idea. But he was one of those men who can blunt a conflict by misrepresenting their judgement of the opposing themes of it. If it had been pointed out to him that a growing girl might be endangered by regular, unsupervised contact with a man whose wife left him unsatisfied, he would certainly have replied that he could rely on his daughter, a man like K. could never be a danger to her, and his friend was incapable in himself of any such intentions. Or he would have said that Dora was still a child, and K. treated her as a child. In fact, however, each of the two men avoided drawing any conclusions from the conduct of the other that might be unwelcome to his own desires. For a year, Herr K. was able to send Dora flowers every day while he was in the same town, use every opportunity to make her expensive presents, and spend all his free time in her company without her parents seeing anything like sexual advances in his conduct.

If a well-founded chain of ideas to which no objection can be made emerges in psychoanalytic treatment, it is probably awkward for the doctor, whom his patient may ask: 'But surely all that is correct and true? If I told you that, what do you want to change about it?' It soon becomes clear that such ideas on the patient's part, which are not open to analysis, are being used to cover up other ideas that prefer to elude criticism and the conscious mind. A series of accusations of other people leads us to assume a series of self-accusations of the same nature. This way of fending off a self-accusation by accusing another person of the same thing has something undeniably automatic about it. Its model is the verbal duels of children who without a moment's thought reply, 'You're the liar!' if accused of lying themselves. An adult in search of a cutting riposte would look for some real vulnerability in his adversary, and not lay the main emphasis on repeating the original accusation. In paranoia, projection of the accusation on someone else without changing the content, and thus without reference to reality, is evident as a delusion.

Dora's accusations of her father were shored up by self-accusations of the same nature, like mirror images, as we can show in details: she was right to think that her father did not want to understand Herr K.'s conduct towards his daughter, so as not to have his relationship with Frau K. disturbed. She had done exactly the same. She had made herself an accomplice to that relationship, rejecting every indication illustrating its true nature. Only after the episode by the lake was she clear about it, and her stern demands of her father dated from the same time. All through the years before it, she had encouraged her father's contact with Frau K. in every possible way. She never went to see Frau K. when she thought her father would be there. She knew that then the children would have been sent out, and arranged her own movements so as to meet them and take them for a walk. There had been one person in the house who tried to open her eyes to her father's relationship with Frau K. and turn her against the woman. This was Dora's last governess, an older and very well-read young woman of liberal views.[1] For some time teacher and pupil got on

[1] As for this governess, who read many books on sexual life and such subjects, and talked to the girl about them, but candidly asked her not to mention such things to her parents, because you could not know what point of view they would take—for some time I looked for the source of all Dora's secret knowledge in that young woman, and I may not have been entirely wrong.

very well with one another, until Dora suddenly turned against her governess and insisted on her being dismissed. As long as the governess had any influence, she used it to turn Dora against Frau K. She suggested to Dora's mother that it was undignified for her to tolerate such intimacy on her husband's part with another woman, and pointed out all the conspicuous aspects of their relationship to Dora as well. Her efforts were in vain; Dora still had affectionate feelings for Frau K., and would not hear of any reason why her father's contact with her might be objectionable. On the other hand, she had a very good idea of the motives impelling her governess. Blind in one way, she was sharp-sighted enough in another. She saw that the governess was in love with her Papa. When he was present, she seemed an entirely different person, and could be amusing and helpful. At the time when the family was living in the town where he had his factory, and Frau K. was not on the horizon, she tried turning Dora against her Mama, as the rival she now had to fear. Dora did not hold this against her. She was annoyed only when she realized that she herself was of no real importance to the governess, and the affection that the latter had shown her was in fact for the benefit of her Papa. When her Papa was away from the manufacturing town, the governess had no time for Dora, did not want to go for walks with her, and was not interested in her studies. As soon as Papa was back from B., she became helpful and serviceable again. Then Dora dropped her.

However, the unfortunate young woman had cast an unwelcome but clear light on one aspect of Dora's own behaviour. Dora had sometimes made use of Herr K.'s children exactly as the governess had made use of her. She took the place of a mother with them, taught them, took them out, gave them a complete substitute for their own mother's lack of interest in them. Herr and Frau K. had often discussed divorce, but nothing came of it, because Herr K., who was a loving father, did not want to lose touch with either of the two children. Their common interest in the children had been a link between Herr K. and Dora from the first. To Dora, her concern for the children was obviously a cover intended to hide something else from herself and other people.

Her conduct towards the children, as explained by the governess's conduct to her, led to the same conclusion as did her tacit consent to her father's relationship with Frau K., which was that all these years she had been in love with Herr K. herself. When I put this conclusion into words, she rejected it. She did tell me immediately that other people, for instance a girl cousin who came to stay with the family for a while in B., had told her, 'You're crazy about that man,' but she herself said she couldn't recollect any such feelings. Later, when the wealth of material that was emerging made denial more difficult, she admitted that she could have been in love with Herr K. in B., but after the scene beside the lake all that was over.[1] At any rate, it was certain that the accusation of having been deaf to the call of duties that could not be shrugged off and arranging things to suit her own enamoured emotions, the very accusation she levelled against her father, rebounded on herself.[2]

The other accusation, that her father used his ill-health as a pretext and a means of getting what he wanted, once again coincides with a certain part of her own secret history. One day she complained of what she said was a new symptom, sharp stomach-aches, and when I asked, 'Whose stomach-aches are you imitating?' I had hit the mark. The day before, she had visited her cousins, her late aunt's daughters. The younger had become engaged, and as a result the elder contracted stomach-pains and had to be taken to the resort of Semmering* to convalesce. She said she thought the elder girl, who always had some disorder, did it only out of envy when she wanted to get her own way in something, and now she wanted to leave home so as not to witness her sister's happiness.[3] Dora's own stomach-aches, however, expressed the fact that she was identifying with her elder cousin, who had been accused of malingering, whether because she too

---

[1] See the second dream.
[2] Here the question arises: if Dora loved Herr K., how do we account for her rejection of him in the scene beside the lake, or at least the brutality of that rejection, which suggests bitterness? How could a girl in love see his advances, which—as we shall hear later—were by no means crude or offensive, as an insult?
[3] An everyday event among sisters.

envied the happier girl her love, or because she saw her own fate
reflected in that of the elder sister, whose own love-affair had
ended unhappily not long ago.[1] She had also been able to see how
usefully illness can be exploited by observing Frau K. Herr K.
was away travelling for part of the year; whenever he came home
he found his wife unwell, when only a day before, as Dora knew,
there had been nothing wrong with her. Dora realized that the
presence of her husband made his wife feel ill, and that illness was
welcome to her because it meant that she could avoid the marital
duties she disliked. A comment by Dora on her own oscillation
between illness and health during the first years she spent as a
young girl in B.—she suddenly came out with it at this point—
made me assume that her own circumstances were to be regarded
as depending on factors similar to Frau K.'s. It is a rule in the
technique of psychoanalysis that an internal but still concealed
connection is shown by the contiguity and proximity in time of
ideas, in the same way as the fact that writing the letters *a* and *b*
side by side makes them form the syllable *ab*. Dora had suffered a
great many attacks of coughing with loss of voice; could the presence or absence of the beloved have had an influence on the coming and fading of her symptoms of sickness? If that were the case,
it must be possible to find a tell-tale correspondence somewhere.
I asked what the average duration of these attacks had been. About
three to six weeks. How long, I also asked, had Herr K.'s absences
lasted? She had to admit: also between three and six weeks. So
with her sickness, she was demonstrating her love for K., just as
his wife was demonstrating her dislike for him in the same way.
We have only to suppose that she and his wife acted in opposite
ways; Dora had been ill when he was away, and was healthy when
he came back. It did really seem to be like that, at least for the first
period during which she suffered these attacks; later she probably
felt it necessary to blur the coincidence of her sickness and the
absence of the man she secretly loved, so that the secret was not
given away by its consistency. However, the duration of an attack
remained as a record of its original significance.

[1] I shall come, later, to the further conclusion I drew from the stomach-aches.

I remembered that in the past, I had seen and heard at the Charcot clinic* that in people with hysterical mutism, writing became a vicarious substitute for speech. They wrote more fluently, faster, and better than others, and better than they themselves used to. That had been the case with Dora. In the first days of her aphonia she found that 'writing was always particularly easy for her'. This peculiarity, expressing a physiological substitute function created by the need for it, did not really call for any psychological explanation, but it was remarkable that such an explanation was readily available. Herr K. wrote to her at length about his travels and sent picture-postcards. It sometimes happened that he told no one else the date of his return, and it came as a surprise to his wife. Corresponding with someone who is absent, and to whom you cannot speak, is as obvious as trying to make yourself understood by writing when you have lost your voice. Dora's aphonia thus allowed the following symbolic interpretation: when the beloved was away she refrained from speaking. The fact that she could not speak to *him* had lost its value. Instead, writing acquired significance as the only means of getting in touch with the absent beloved.

Shall I now claim that in all cases of periodically occurring aphonia we must diagnose the existence of a beloved person who at times is not physically present? I certainly do not intend to do that. The determination of the symptom in Dora's case is too specific for us to postulate the frequent recurrence of what is an accidental aetiology. However, what value does such an explanation of aphonia have in this case? Have we not, rather, let ourselves be deceived by a witty play on words? I think not. Here we must remember the question so often put of whether the symptoms of hysteria are psychological or somatic in origin, and whether, if the former explanation is admitted, they are all necessarily caused by psychological factors. This question, like so many others that we see scholars unsuccessfully trying to resolve, is inadequate. The real facts of the matter are not covered by the alternative it postulates. As far as I can see, every hysterical symptom requires a contribution from both sides. It cannot arise without a certain *somatic compliance*, performed by means of a normal or abnormal process in one or other of the organs of the body. It occurs only once—and an ability to recur is a characteristic of a hysterical symptom—if it has no psychological significance, no *meaning*. That meaning is not inherent in the hysterical symptom; it is conferred on it, so to speak amalgamated with it, and it can be different in every case, depending on the nature of the repressed thought struggling for expression. However, a whole series of factors are at work to ensure that the connections between unconscious thoughts and the somatic processes available to them as a means of expression are less arbitrary and approach several typical links. For therapy, the determinations present in the accidental psychological material are the more important; the symptoms are resolved by exploration of their psychological meaning. If we have then cleared away what can be removed by psychoanalysis, we can entertain all kinds of probably correct ideas about the foundations of the somatic symptoms, which are usually constitutional and organic. Here we will not confine ourselves to psychoanalytical interpretation of Dora's coughing and aphonia, but will find the organic factor behind them from which the 'somatic compliance' arose for the expression of her affection for a temporarily absent beloved. And if the connection between the symptomatic expression and the content of unconscious thought in this case is to appear skilful and ingeniously put into practice, we shall be glad to hear that it can make the same impression in every other case, every other example.

I am prepared to hear at this point that it is only moderately useful if, thanks to psychoanalysis, we no longer try to find a solution to the riddle of hysteria in the 'particular lability of the molecules of the nerves' or the possibility of hypnoid states, but seek it in somatic compliance.

However, I would counter that by emphasizing that the riddle is not only partially distanced by that means, it is also partially reduced. We are no longer looking at the riddle as a whole, but at that part of it where the particular character of hysteria resides *as distinct* from other psychoneuroses. Psychological processes run the same course in all psychoneuroses, and only after that do we have to consider the somatic compliance that gives the unconscious psychological processes an escape-route into physical expression. Where that factor is not available, the patient's whole state of mind becomes something other than a hysterical symptom, and yet is something related to it: a phobia, maybe, or an obsessive idea—in short, a psychological symptom.

Let me return to the way in which Dora accused her father of simulating his medical disorders. We soon saw that not only did that match her self-accusations of past disorders, but also some in the present. Here it is usually up to the doctor to guess—and complete—what analysis only hints at. I had to point out to my patient that her present state of illness had tendentious motives, just like those she saw in Frau K. There was no doubt that she had some end in view and hoped to achieve it through illness. That end could only be to detach her father from Frau K. She could not do it by pleading and arguments; perhaps she might get somewhere by alarming her father (remember the farewell letter), arousing his pity (by means of her attacks of faintness), and if none of this was any good, she would at least get her revenge on him. She probably knew, I said, how much he loved her, and she knew that tears came into his eyes whenever he was asked how his daughter was. I was convinced, I added, that she would be better at once if her father said that he was sacrificing Frau K. to her health. I hoped that he would not be persuaded to do so, because then she would have seen what a strong weapon she had in her hands, and would certainly not shrink from exploiting all the possibilities of illness on every future occasion. However, if her father did not give in to her, I felt sure that she would not abandon her invalid status so easily.

I will pass over the details of the way in which it turned out that I was entirely correct in all this, and instead will make some general remarks about the motives for illness in hysteria. The motives for illness are to be clearly distinguished from the opportunities of it, the material from which the symptoms are manufactured. They have no part in the formation of symptoms and are not present at the beginning of the illness; they occur only as a secondary feature, but not until they do is the illness fully developed.[1] One can always count on its being present in every case where there is genuine suffering lasting for some time. The symptom is first and foremost an unwelcome guest in the patient's psychological life; it has every disadvantage, and therefore seems to disappear easily of its own accord under the influence of passing time. At first it has no usefulness in the economy of the psyche, but it very often acquires secondary usefulness; some kind of psychological current finds it convenient to make use of the symptom, and thus it gains a *secondary function* and is, as it were, anchored in the mind. Anyone trying to cure the patient will then, to his surprise, encounter great resistance, teaching him that the invalid is not entirely serious in wishing to be better.[2] Take a manual labourer, for instance a roofer, who is crippled after falling from a height and now keeps himself alive by begging in the street. Suppose someone appears in the character of a miracle-worker and promises to make his lame leg straight so that he can walk on it again. I do not think we could count on seeing any expression of particular delight on his face. He will certainly have felt very unhappy when he first suffered his injury, realizing that he would never be able to work again and must either starve or live on charity. Since then, however, what put him out of a job has become his source of income; he lives from his disability. Take that away from him, and he may be entirely helpless; he has forgotten his old trade by now,

---

[1] (Added in 1923.) This is not entirely correct. The thesis that such motives are not present at the beginning of the illness and occur only as a secondary feature cannot be maintained. In what follows that remark, motives for illness are mentioned that are present before the disorder sets in, and are partly responsible for it. I later did the facts of the matter more justice by introducing the distinction between *primary and secondary advantages gained by illness.* The motive for illness is always the intention of gaining an advantage. For the secondary advantage, what I said in the rest of this section holds good. However, a primary advantage can be discerned in every neurotic malady. Falling ill, in the first place, spares the sufferer psychic effort, and turns out to be economically the most convenient solution in the case of mental conflict (*flight into illness*), although in most cases the impracticability of such a solution becomes very clear later. This part of the primary advantage of illness can be described as the *inner*, psychological part; it is, so to speak, constant. In addition, external factors, such as the situation cited of a woman kept in subjection by her husband, can give rise to motives for illness, thus constituting the *external* part of the primary advantage of illness.

[2] Arthur Schnitzler, a writer who is also a doctor, has given very cogent expression to this phenomenon in his *Paracelsus.**

got out of the habit of working, he has accustomed himself to idleness and perhaps to heavy drinking too.

Motives for illness often begin to show themselves in childhood. A little girl hungry for love, unwilling to share her parents' affection with her siblings, will notice that it is directed on her with full force again if her parents are anxious because she is sick. Now she has a means of enticing their love her way, and she will use it as soon as she has the psychic material to make herself ill at her disposal. Once she is a woman, and in contrast to the demands of her childhood is married to a man who shows little consideration for her, suppresses her own will, makes unsparing use of her power to work, and gives her neither affection nor presents, illness becomes her only weapon for staking her own claim on life. It offers the leisure she longed for, forces her husband to devote money and consideration to her that he would not have given when she was healthy, it obliges him to treat her with care if she gets better, because otherwise she may always relapse. Her illness, apparently unwanted if seen objectively, as the doctor treating her will vouch, makes it possible for her to use a method that she found effective as a child without consciously blaming herself for it.

And yet her illness is intentional! As a rule, states of illness are determined by a certain person, so that if that person goes away so does the illness. The most banal and unfeeling opinion of a hysteric's illness, heard expressed by nurses and her untrained relations alike, is correct in a certain sense. It is true that even a bed-ridden woman would jump up if fire broke out in the room, an over-indulged woman would forget all her own suffering if a child of hers fell dangerously ill or a catastrophe threatened the stability of her house. All of those who speak of the sick like this are right up to that point, but they ignore the psychological difference between the conscious and the unconscious mind, permissible in a child but inappropriate in an adult. Consequently no assurances that it is only a matter of will-power, and no encouragement or scolding, will do the sick woman any good. We have to begin by trying to convince the patient herself of the existence of her intention to be ill by the circuitous method of analysis.

The weak point of every therapy used to treat hysteria in general, including psychoanalytical therapy, lies in opposing the motives for illness. Fate has an easier task here in not having to attack either the constitution or the pathogenic material of a patient; it removes a motive for being ill, and the patient is temporarily or perhaps even permanently free of his disorder. In treating hysteria, we doctors would have to accept many fewer miraculous cures and symptoms that spontaneously disappear if we could get an insight more often into our patients' secret but vital interests! A period of waiting has run its course, consideration need no longer be taken for someone else, external events have brought fundamental change into a situation, and the patient's hitherto persistent suffering has suddenly gone away, apparently spontaneously, but in fact because the strongest motive for it, one of its uses in the patient's life, has been removed.

Motives shoring up illness are likely to be found in all fully developed cases. However, some cases have purely internal motives, for instance, self-punishment, involving repentance and penance. The therapeutic task is then easier to resolve, for instance, when the illness is seen in connection with the attainment of some external aim. Dora's aim, obviously, was to soften her father's attitude and induce him to leave Frau K.

Nothing he did, as it happens, seemed to make her feel so bitter as his readiness to take the lakeside scene as the creation of her own imagination. She was beside herself when she thought that she was believed to have been deluding herself over it. I was baffled for a long time as I tried to work out what self-accusation was hidden behind her passionate rejection of that explanation. It was right to assume some hidden factor behind it, for an accusation that misses its mark does not leave lasting resentment. On the other hand, I came to the conclusion that Dora's story must correspond to the truth. After she had understood what Herr K.'s intentions were, she did not let him explain himself but slapped his face and ran away. Her conduct probably appeared to Herr K. at the time, when he was left behind, as inexplicable as it does to us, for he must long ago have concluded, from innumerable little signs, that he could be sure of the girl's feeling for him. In discussion of the second dream, we shall find the answer to that puzzle and also the reason for self-accusation that we had looked for.

When Dora's complaints of her father recurred with tedious monotony, and she went on coughing, it made me think it was to him that the significance of that symptom related. In fact the features that I usually consider necessary for an explanation of symptoms were far from being present. According to a rule that I have found confirmed again and again, although I have not felt bold enough before to call it a general rule, a symptom is the presentation—or realization—of a fantasy with a sexual content, that is to say, a sexual situation. Or I would do better to say, at least *one* of the meanings of a symptom corresponds to the presentation of a sexual fantasy, while there is no such limit to the content of its other meanings. When you enter the field of psychoanalytical work, you very soon find out that a symptom has more than one meaning, and serves to present several unconscious thought processes at the same time. I would like to add that, in my opinion, a single unconscious thought process or fantasy is hardly ever enough to generate a symptom on its own.

I very soon had an opportunity to interpret Dora's nervous coughing as the outcome of a fantasized sexual situation. When she pointed out yet again that Frau K. loved Papa only because he was *a man of means*, I could tell from certain circumstances affecting her use of this expression, which I shall pass over here as I do with most of what is purely technical in the process of analysis, that the opposite of this remark lay concealed behind it: her father was *not a man of means*. This could only be meant sexually; while her father might be a man of means in the sense of prosperity, he had no means of making an impression as a man, that is to say, he was impotent. When she confirmed this interpretation as something of which she was aware, I suggested to her that she was contradicting herself if she said, on the one hand, that her father's relationship with Frau K. was an ordinary love-affair, but on the other hand claimed that he was impotent and unable to exploit such a relationship. Her answer clearly showed that she did not have to acknowledge the contradiction. She said she knew very well that there was more than one way of achieving sexual satisfaction. However, she could not say what the source of her knowledge was. When I went on to ask whether she meant making use of human organs other than the genitals for sexual intercourse, she said yes, and I was able to continue that train of thought: then she had in mind those parts of her body that were in an inflamed state (her throat, her oral cavity). She would not, in fact, admit as much, but she did not need to be able to explain it in full for the symptom to appear. However, the corollary was irrefutable: her spasmodic coughing, which as usual was set off by a tickling in her throat, represented a situation of sexual satisfaction *per os** between the two people whose amorous relationship was constantly on her mind. The fact that, very soon after I had provided an explanation for her coughing, to which she listened without comment, the cough disappeared was of course in tune with that explanation, but we did not want to dwell too much on this change because it had often occurred spontaneously before.

This part of the analysis may have displeased and horrified a medical reader, quite apart from the disbelief that he is free to entertain, but I am ready to test both reactions at this point to find out if they are justified. I think displeasure may be motivated by my venturing to discuss such delicate and disgusting subjects with a young girl, or indeed any woman who has reached the age of sexual maturity. Horror would probably be evoked by the possibility that a virginal girl could know and fantasize about such practices. I would advise moderation and circumspect thought on both points. There is no reason for either to arouse indignation. One can discuss all sexual matters with girls and women, without harming them or casting any aspersions on their virtue, if one adopts, first, a certain way of tackling the subject, and secondly if one can convince them that it is necessary to do so. In the same circumstances a gynaecologist can get them to expose all parts of their bodies to him. The best way of discussing the subject is in a dry, factual manner that, at the same time, is very far from the prurience with which women and girls are used to hearing such subjects discussed in 'society'. I give organs and processes their technical names, and impart the meanings of those names if they happen to be unknown. *J'appelle un chat un chat.** I have heard of those both inside and outside the medical profession who are scandalized by a method of therapy in which such conversations take place, and who seem to envy me or my patients the stimulation that they expect to be felt. But I know the respectable attitudes of such gentlemen too well to be annoyed. I will avoid the temptation to write a satire. I will mention only that I frequently have the satisfaction of hearing a woman patient who at first did not find it easy to be frank about sexual matters say later, 'Your cure is much less improper than the conversation of Herr X.!'

We have to be convinced of the inevitability of touching on sexual subjects before we undertake to treat a case of hysteria, or at least be prepared to learn about it from experience. *Pour faire une omelette il faut casser des oeufs*, we reflect: to make an omelette you must break eggs. The patients themselves are easily convinced; there are only too many opportunities to convince them in the course of treatment. We need not reproach ourselves for discussing the facts of normal or abnormal sexual life with them. If we use some circumspection, we are merely bringing to the conscious mind what the unconscious mind knows already, and the efficacy of the cure rests entirely on the realization that the affective influences of an unconscious idea are stronger than those of a conscious idea, and because they cannot be kept in check are more harmful. We are never in danger of corrupting an inexperienced girl; where there is no knowledge of sexual matters in the unconscious mind, no hysterical symptoms can develop. Where we find hysteria, we cannot speak of 'innocence of thought' in the sense meant by a girl's parents and teachers. I have convinced myself that this precept holds good, without exception, in children of ten, twelve, and fourteen, boys and girls alike.

As for the second emotional reaction, directed this time not at me but at the patient, assuming that I am right about her—the reaction of horror at the perverse character of her fantasies—I would like to emphasize that such vehement passion is inappropriate in a medical verdict. I also think it superfluous, among other things, for a doctor writing about the aberrations of sexual drives to take every opportunity of expressing his personal abhorrence of such repellent matters in the text. We have here a fact to which, it is to be hoped, we can accustom ourselves by suppressing our own tastes. We must be able to discuss, without any indignation, what we call sexual perversions, in which the usual border of the sexual function is crossed with regard to areas of the body and to sexual objects. Even the uncertainty of the limits of what may be called normal sexual life in different races and at different periods ought to cool the indignant down. We must not forget that what seems to us the most repellent of these perversions, sexual love between men, was not only tolerated in a people as culturally superior to us as the ancient Greeks, it also performed an important role in society. All of us, in our own sexual lives, cross the narrow boundary of what we call normal a little way in one direction or another. Perversions are neither bestial nor degenerate as that word is emotionally used. They are developments of embryonic ideas present in the undifferentiated sexual disposition of children, and their suppression or elevation to a higher, non-sexual purpose—their *sublimation*—determines the release of powers that are behind a considerable number of our cultural achievements. Where someone has *become* coarse and clearly perverse, we can more correctly say that he has *remained* so, he represents a state of *arrested development*. Psychoneurotics are all people with strongly developed tendencies that have been repressed in the course of development and have become unconscious and perverse. Their unconscious fantasies therefore clearly have the same content as the established actions of the perverse, even if they have never read Krafft-Ebing's *Psychopathia sexualis*,* which the naive blame for the emergence of perverse tendencies. Psychoneuroses, so to speak, are the *negative* of perversions. In neurotics their sexual disposition, which also expresses hereditary factors, works together with accidental influences to disturb the development of normal sexuality. A torrent of water that finds an obstacle in its way in one riverbed will be forced back into older channels that it is supposed to have left behind. The driving forces for the formation of hysterical symptoms are made available not only by the repression of normal sexuality but also by unconscious perverse promptings.[1]

The less repellent of what are called sexual perversions are the most common among the general population, as everyone knows apart from the medical author who writes on this subject. Or rather, the medical author knows it too, but he tries to forget it the moment he picks up a pen to write about it. So it is not surprising if my patient, a hysteric nearly nineteen years old, who had heard of such a sexual practice as sucking the penis, developed an unconscious fantasy along the same lines, and expressed it by the sensation of a tickle in the throat and by coughing. Nor would it be surprising if she had developed such a fantasy without any external explanation for it, as I have found certainly happened with some other woman patients. In her case the somatic prerequisite for the independent creation of a fantasy in this way, one congruent with a perverse act, was the noteworthy fact that as a child she had been a thumb-sucker. Her father also remembered that he had weaned her of the habit when it went on until she was four or five. Dora herself had a clear image from her early childhood in her memory; she recollected sitting in a corner on the floor, sucking her left thumb, while with her right hand she pulled her brother's earlobe as he sat quietly beside her. This is the kind of complete self-satisfaction engendered by sucking that I have had described to me by other patients who later suffered from loss of sensation and hysteria. I heard an anecdote from one of them that casts a bright light on the origin of this curious habit. That young woman, who had never given up the habit of thumb-sucking at all, saw herself, in a childhood memory, suckling at her wet-nurse's breast while rhythmically pulling the nurse's earlobe. I do not think anyone will dispute that the mucous membrane of the lips and mouth can be called a primary *erogenous* zone, since it has retained part of that significance in kissing, which is regarded as normal. Early full activation of this erogenous zone, then, is the

---

[1] These lines about sexual perversions were written several years before the excellent study by I. Bloch (*Beiträge zur Ätiologie der Psychopathia sexualis* [*Contributions to the Aetiology of the Psychopathia sexualis*], 1902 and 1903). See also my book, published this year (1905), *Three Essays on the Theory of Sexuality* [SE vii].

condition for later somatic arousal of the mucous membrane area,
beginning with the lips. If at a time when it has been recognized
that the real sexual object is the penis, there are conditions that
will further heighten the still existing erogenous oral area, it does
not take much creative force to substitute that real sexual object
for the nipple and the fingers acting vicariously for it, and place it
in a situation where the result will be satisfaction. So what is
regarded as a perverse and offensive fantasy of sucking the penis
has the most harmless of origins; it is a reworking of what we
could call a prehistoric impression of sucking at the mother's or
nurse's breast, which has often been revived by contact with
children being suckled. Usually the cow's udder has served as a
suitable intermediate image between the nipple and the penis.

The interpretation of Dora's throat symptoms mentioned above
can also give rise to another point. We may wonder how this
fantasized sexual situation can be reconciled with the other observation, the fact that the coming and going of symptoms of illness
imitate the presence and absence of a beloved man, thus expressing, if we take the woman's actions into account, this train of
thought: if I were his wife, I would love him in a very different
way—I would be ill (with longing, perhaps) when he goes away,
and healthy (with happiness) when he is back at home. I must
answer that question according to my experiences of resolving
hysterical symptoms: it is not necessary for the various meanings
of a symptom to agree with one another, that is, to be complementary. It is enough for the connection between them to be made by
the subject that has given rise to all the different fantasies. In our
present case such a complementary relation is not excluded; one
meaning applies more to the coughing, the other to the aphonia
and the course of events producing those conditions. A more
probing analysis would probably have brought to light more
details intellectually defining the illness. We have already seen that
a symptom can regularly be capable of having several *simultaneous*
meanings; let us now add that it can be capable of several *successive*
meanings. Over the years, the symptom can change one of its
meanings, or its main meaning, or the main role can pass from one

meaning to another. A conservative feature, so to speak, in the character of neurosis is that once formed, a symptom is retained wherever possible, even if the unconscious idea that it expressed has lost its meaning. However, it is easy to explain this tendency as mechanical retention of the symptom: creating a symptom of that kind is such hard work, transferring a purely psychological emotion into physical form, something that I have called *conversion*, depends so much on favourable circumstances, a somatic compliance such as is needed for conversion is so difficult to achieve, that the urge to discharge excitement from the unconscious mind may lead to making do with a means of discharge that is already known. Creating associations between a new idea requiring discharge, and the old one that no longer requires it, seems much easier than creating a new conversion. On a path already trodden, excitement streams from its new source to the old means of discharging it, and the symptom, as the Gospels put it, is like putting new wine into old bottles.* If, after these remarks, the somatic part of the hysterical symptom seems to be the more enduring, harder to replace, and the psychological part is volatile, more easily replaced, we do not have to deduce that there was any ranking order between the two parts. For psychotherapy, however, the psychological part is the more important.

The constant recurrence of Dora's idea of her father's relationship to Frau K. offered me an opportunity to make another important discovery in her analysis.

Such a train of thought can be called over-strong, or rather *reinforced*, or *supervalent* in Wernicke's* sense of that word. In spite of its apparently correct content it turns out to be morbid because of its unique peculiarity: in the face of all conscious and arbitrary efforts of the mind, it cannot be deconstructed or disposed of. In a normal train of thought, however intensive, you finally reach the end of it. Dora was aware, correctly, that her thoughts about her Papa called for special assessment. 'I can't think of anything else,' she repeatedly complained. 'My brother tells me that as Papa's children we have no right to criticize what he does. So we ought not to feel concern, perhaps we should even be glad that he has found a woman to whom he can be truly attached, since Mama doesn't understand him. I can see that, and I would like to think as my brother does, but I can't. I can't forgive Papa.'[1]

What is to be done about such a supervalent idea, once we have heard the conscious reasons for it as well as the unsuccessful objections to those reasons? We tell ourselves *that this over-strong train of thought owes its reinforcement to the unconscious mind.* Thinking cannot resolve it, either because it is rooted in unconscious, suppressed material, or because another unconscious idea is hidden behind it. The latter is usually its precise opposite. Opposites are always closely linked, and often paired so that while *one idea is excessively conscious, its corresponding opposite is repressed and unconscious.* This relationship is a sign of successful repression. Repression is frequently contrived in such a way that the opposite of the idea to be repressed is excessively reinforced. I call this the reinforcement of reaction, and I call the idea claiming excessive emphasis in the conscious mind, which, like a prejudice cannot be broken down, an *idea of reaction.* The two ideas are then related roughly like a pair of astatic or unstable needles. With a certain surplus intensity, the idea of reaction keeps the offensive factor at bay and withheld from conscious thought; however, it is muted in the process itself, and protected from the conscious work of thought. Bringing the repressed opposite into the conscious mind, therefore, is the way to deprive the over-strong idea of its reinforcement.

We must not exclude from our expectations a case where we are looking at not one of the two reasons for supervalent thought but rivalry between both. There can also be other complications, but they are easily accommodated.

In the example offered to us by Dora, let us first try assuming that the origin of her compulsive concern with her father's relationship with Frau K. was unknown to Dora herself, because it is in

---

[1] A supervalent idea of this kind, together with deep depression, is often the only sign of a state of sickness that is usually called melancholia, but like a case of hysteria it can be resolved by psychoanalysis.

the field of the unconscious. It is not difficult to guess, from the circumstances and her symptoms. Her conduct obviously went far beyond the usual role of a daughter; she felt and acted more like a jealous wife, an attitude that would have been understandable in her mother. By issuing an ultimatum—'Either her or me'—as well as the scenes in which she indulged and her hints threatening suicide, she was clearly putting herself in her mother's place. If I am right in supposing that the fantasy of a sexual situation is behind her coughing, then with that cough she was putting herself in the place of Frau K. She thus identified with both of the women loved by her father, now and in the past. It is logical to conclude that her affection for her father was stronger than she knew or would have liked to admit: that she was in love with her father.

I have learnt to see such unconscious bonds of love between father and daughter, mother and son, manifested by their abnormal consequences, as the revival of early infantile stirrings of emotion. Elsewhere,[1] I have explained the way in which the sexual attraction between parents and children makes itself felt at an early stage, and have cited the story of Oedipus* as a poetic reworking of the typical features of these relationships. Early attraction of a daughter to her father and a son to his mother, something of which most people will probably find a clear trace in themselves, is bound to be felt more intensely from the first by children with a constitutional tendency towards neurosis who are precocious and hungry for love. We then find that influences which need not be discussed here come into play, fixating the rudimentary feeling of love, or reinforcing it so strongly that, whether in childhood or not until puberty, it becomes something that resembles sexual love, and like sexual love, makes demands on the libido.[2] In Dora's case, her external circumstances were far from unfavourable to such an assumption. Her disposition had always drawn her to her father; his many illnesses were bound to

[1] In *The Interpretation of Dreams*, and in the third of the *Essays on the Theory of Sexuality*.

[2] The deciding factor here is probably the early appearance of true genital sensations, whether spontaneous or aroused by seduction and masturbation.

increase her love for him; in a number of them no one but Dora
was allowed to perform the little services of nursing for him.
Proud of her intelligence, which was evident early, he had made
her his confidante even as a child. When Frau K. appeared on the
scene, it was not really her mother but Dora herself who found
that more than one of her positions had been usurped.

When I told Dora I was assuming that her affection for her
father had taken on the full character of amorous love, she gave
her usual answer—'I don't remember anything like that'—but
immediately told me of something similar in her cousin on her
mother's side, a girl of seven, in whom she thought she often saw
features of her own childhood reflected. The child had witnessed,
not for the first time, an angry altercation between her parents,
and had whispered to Dora, when she came to visit, 'You've no
idea how much I hate that person!' while pointing to her mother.
'If she dies some day I'm going to marry Papa!' I am used to seeing
such incidents, which have features harmonizing with the content
of my claim, a confirmation rising from the unconscious. We cannot expect the unconscious mind to say yes in any other way, and
there is no such thing as an unconscious no.[1]

For years there was no expression of any amorous feelings for her
father; indeed, she was on very cordial terms for a long time with
the very woman who had displaced her in her father's affections,
and as we know from her self-accusations, she had even encouraged the relationship with her father. So her love had recently
been revived, and if that was the case we must ask why it happened. It was obviously a reaction symptom in order to repress
something else that was still powerfully at work in her unconscious mind. As things were, I thought first and foremost that love
for Herr K. was what must be repressed. I had to assume that she
was still in love with him, but that the scene by the lake—for
whatever unknown reasons—set up strong resistance to such an

---

[1] (Added in 1923.) Another very curious and very reliable form of confirmation from
the unconscious mind, which I did not yet know when I wrote this work, is when a
patient cries, 'I wasn't thinking of that,' or, 'I didn't think of that.' We can translate this
remark as: Yes, but that was not in my conscious mind.

idea, and the girl then revived and reinforced her old love for her father, so that the first love of her adolescent years, now painful for her to remember, would no longer be present in her consciousness. Then I also gained an insight into a conflict very likely to shake the girl's mental life. On the one hand she was sorry to have turned down the man's advances, she longed for his person and the small signs of his affection; on the other hand, there were strong reasons opposing such tender and longing emotions, among which it was easy to detect her pride. So she had persuaded herself that she wanted no more to do with Herr K.—that was the advantage she gained from this typical process of repression— and yet to protect herself against the amorous feelings always pressing in on her conscious mind, she had to call on her childish love for her father and exaggerate it. However, there seemed to be another possible determination of the way she had been dominated almost entirely by bitter jealousy.[1]

I was not at all surprised to find that this idea aroused outright contradiction in Dora. The denial that you hear from patients after you confront their conscious perception with repressed ideas confirms the repression and its firm establishment, and so to speak tests its strength. If we take that denial not as the expression of impartial judgement, of which the patient is incapable, but pass over it and continue work, the first evidence that 'No' in such a case means the 'Yes' you want to find will soon emerge. She admitted that she could not be quite as angry with Herr K. as he deserved. She said that she had met Herr K. in the street one day, while she was walking with a girl cousin who did not know him. The cousin suddenly cried, 'Dora, what's the matter with you? You're as white as a sheet!' She had not felt herself changing colour, but I told her that changes of facial expression, and signs of emotion, obey the unconscious rather than the conscious mind, and give away more about the former.[2] On another occasion, after several days of steady cheerfulness, she came to see me in a very bad temper and was unable to explain it. She was in such a horrid mood, she said; it was her uncle's birthday and she couldn't bring

[1] As we shall soon see below.
[2] Cf. Schiller's lines: 'Calmly I can see you come, | Calmly see you go.'*

herself to wish him happiness, she didn't know why. My skills of interpretation were blunt that day; I let her talk on, and she suddenly remembered that it was also Herr K.'s birthday, a fact that I did not hesitate to turn against her. Now it was not difficult to explain why all the presents she received on her own birthday a few days earlier had given her no pleasure. There was no present from Herr K., and his had obviously been the one she really would have treasured.

Meanwhile, she stuck to her denial of my claims for a long time, until towards the end of the analysis evidence showing that I was right emerged.

Now I must mention another complication, to which I certainly would not devote space if I were a writer inventing such a state of mind for a novella, instead of analysing it as a doctor. The factor that I am about to mention can only dim and blur the beauties of the conflict—just the thing for literature—that we may assume was going on in Dora; an author would certainly use his prerogative of censorship, preferring simplicity and ignoring what seems extraneous when he sets up as a psychologist. In reality, however—and I am anxious to describe reality here—motives are complicated, and the accumulation and assembling of psychological states of mind, in short, over-determination, is the rule. Behind Dora's supervalent train of thought about her father's relationship with Frau K. there also lay jealousy of that lady herself—an emotion, then, that could arise only from attraction towards her own sex. It has long been known, and often pointed out, that in boys and girls who have reached puberty clear signs of attraction towards their own sex are normally observed. A schoolgirl's enthusiastic friendship for another, with vows, kisses, promises of corresponding for ever, and all the sensitivity of jealousy, is the usual precursor of her first, more intense attachment to a man. In favourable circumstances the homosexual current often dies down entirely at that point; where her love for a man does not turn out happily, however, it will often be reawakened by her libido in later years and heightened to varying degrees of intensity. If that can easily be established in healthy women, then—and see my earlier comments on the stronger formation of embryonic perversion in neurotics—we shall also expect to find a stronger disposition to homosexuality in the nature of a neurotic. Indeed, this must be so, because I have never psychoanalysed a man or a woman without noting a very significant homosexual current in my patient. Where the sexual libido proper to feelings for a man is firmly repressed in hysterical women and girls, we regularly find that the libido directed vicariously at women is stronger, and has even become partially conscious.

I shall not explore this subject any further here, although it is important and indispensable for the understanding of male hysteria in particular, because Dora's analysis came to an end before it could cast any light on these circumstances in her case. However, I think of the governess with whom she exchanged intimate thoughts until she noticed that she was valued and treated well for her father's sake rather than her own. Then she made sure that the governess left the house. She also dwelt strikingly often on another estrangement, one that was a puzzle to Dora herself. She had always got on particularly well with her other cousin, the girl who later became engaged to be married, and shared all kinds of secrets with her. When her father went back to B. for the first time after his visit to the lake was cut short, and Dora understandably declined to go with him, this cousin was invited to accompany her father, and accepted the invitation. From then on Dora's feelings for her cooled, and she herself was surprised to find how indifferent she now felt to her cousin, although she admitted that she had nothing much to blame her for. These sensitivities made me wonder what her relationship to Frau K. had been before the rift came. I discovered that the young woman and Dora, a girl hardly grown out of childhood, had been very close to each other for years. When Dora stayed with the Ks., she shared Frau K.'s bedroom and her husband had to sleep elsewhere. She was the woman's intimate friend and adviser in all the problems of her married life; there was nothing that they did not discuss. Medea* was happy for Creusa to make friends with her two children as well, and she certainly did nothing to disturb their father's contact with the girl. How Dora herself managed to love a man about whom her dear friend had so many bad things to say is an interesting psychological question, which we can probably answer by observing that ideas, even opposite ideas, live side by side without quarrelling* particularly easily in the unconscious, and such a state of affairs often enough remains the same in the conscious mind.

When Dora spoke of Frau K., she used to praise her 'enchantingly white body' in a tone more suitable to a lover than a defeated rival. On another occasion, sounding melancholy rather than bitter, she told me she was sure that the presents her father brought her had been chosen by Frau K.; she knew her taste. She had been given jewellery that was very like pieces she had seen Frau K. wear, and she had wished out loud that she had something similar. Indeed, I must say that I never heard a harsh or angry word from her about the woman whom, taking into account her supervalent thoughts, she must have seen as the originator of her unhappiness. She acted as if illogically, but her apparent lack of logic was the expression of a current of feeling that complicated matters. For how had the friend she loved so much acted to her? After Dora had complained of Herr K.'s advances, and her father had written asking him to account for himself, he replied at first with professions of respect, and offered to come to the manufacturing town to clear up all misunderstandings. But a few weeks later, when Dora's father spoke to him in B., there was no more talk of respect. He spoke slightingly of Dora, playing his trump card by saying that a girl who read such books and took an interest in such things as she did had no claims on a man's respect. Frau K. must have given her away and blackened her character; it was only to her that Dora had mentioned Mantegazza and sexual subjects. It was the same as with the governess; Frau K. had not loved her for herself either, only on her father's account. Frau K. had sacrificed her without a second thought to preserve her relationship with her father. Perhaps this injury to her feelings struck her more closely and to greater pathogenic effect than the other injury, the one of which she complained to cover it up, the fact that her father had sacrificed her. Did not such persistently maintained amnesia concerning the sources of her improper knowledge point straight to the emotional content of the accusations, and so to her friend's betrayal of her?

I think, then, that I am not wrong in assuming that Dora's supervalent train of thought, concerning her father's relationship with Frau K., was intended to repress not only her once-conscious love for Herr K., but also, and in a deeper sense, her unconscious love for Frau K. Its relation to the other current was that of a direct opposite. She kept telling herself that her Papa had sacrificed her to that woman, demonstrating loudly that she would not allow Frau K. possession of Papa, and thus hiding the opposite, that she could not allow her Papa this woman's love, and had not forgiven the woman whom she herself loved for the disappointment of her treachery. The feminine emotion of jealousy went hand in hand, in Dora's unconscious mind, with the kind of jealousy that a man might have felt. These male, or let us say *gynaecophile*,* currents of emotion, are to be regarded as typical of a hysterical girl's unconscious love-life.

II

THE FIRST DREAM

JUST as we had the prospect of casting light on an obscure part of Dora's childhood by using material that called for analysis, Dora told me that on one night recently she had had a dream, one she had dreamed several times before in exactly the same way. A periodically recurrent dream was, of its very nature, particularly likely to arouse my curiosity; in the interests of treatment, I could contemplate weaving this dream into the context of the analysis. I therefore determined to investigate the dream with especial care.

First dream: *There is a fire in a house,*[1] said Dora, *my father is standing beside my bed and wakes me up. I dress quickly. Mama wants to save her jewel-box, but Papa says: I don't want to burn with both my children because of your jewel-box. We hurry downstairs, and as soon as I am out of the house I wake up.*

As it is a recurrent dream, I naturally ask her when she first had it.—She doesn't know, but she does remember having that dream in L. (the lakeside resort where the scene with Herr K. took place) three nights running, and then she dreamed it again here a few days ago.[2]—The linking of the dream to the events in L. naturally heightens my expectations of finding its meaning. However, first I would like to know the occasion for its latest appearance, and I ask Dora, who has already had some training in the interpretation of dreams by means of a few small examples that we analysed earlier, to take the dream apart and tell me what occurs to her about it.

She says, 'Something that can't be part of it, because it is quite fresh in my mind, and I know I had the dream earlier.'

That doesn't matter, I say, she should go on; it will be her latest relevant reaction to the dream.

---

[1] When I asked, she said that there had never really been a fire in the family house.

[2] It can be shown, from the content, that she first had the dream in L.

'Well, a few days ago Papa had a quarrel with Mama because she locks the dining-room at night. You see, my brother's room has no door of its own leading out of the house; you have to reach it through the dining-room. Papa doesn't like my brother to be locked in at night like that. He said it wouldn't do; some mishap in the night might mean that we had to go out.'

And you related that to the danger of fire?

'Yes.'

Please remember what you say. We may need the exact words. You said that *some mishap in the night might mean that we had to go out.*[1]

Dora has now seen the link between the recent and former occasions for her dream, for she goes on:

'When we went to L. that time, Papa and I, he directly expressed his fear of a fire. We arrived in a violent thunderstorm and saw the little wooden chalet, which had no lightning-conductor. So his fear was natural.'

I am now anxious to trace the connection between the events in L. and the earlier dreams that sounded similar. So I ask: did you have that dream during your first nights in L. or the last ones before you left? That's to say, before or after that scene we know about in the forest? (For I know that incident did not take place on her first day there, and that she stayed on in L. for a few days after it, without letting anyone know what had happened.)

She replies, at first: 'I don't know.' And after a while: 'But I think, after it.'

So now I knew that the dream was a reaction to the experience. But why did it recur three times while she was there? I asked again: How long did you stay in L. after the scene?

'Another four days. Papa and I left on the fifth day.'

I am sure now that the dream was the immediate outcome of that experience with Herr K. You dreamed it first there, no earlier, I said. You only added uncertainty to your memory to blur

---

[1] I pick out those words because they make me wonder. They sound to me ambiguous. Do we not use the same words for certain physical needs? Ambiguous expressions, however, are like points on a railway line; they change the course of association. Switch them to another line than the one that appears in the dream, and you may be on the track along which the ideas you want, still hidden, are moving behind the dream.

the connection.[1] However, the numbers still don't quite seem to me to add up. If you stayed in L. for another four nights, the dream could have recurred four times. Maybe it did?

She does not contradict my statement, but instead of answering my question goes on:[2] 'On the afternoon after our boat trip, when Herr K. and I came back at midday, I lay down as usual on the sofa in the bedroom to take a little nap. I suddenly woke up to find Herr K. standing before me . . .'*

As you saw your Papa standing beside your bed in the dream, then?

'Yes. I asked him to explain what he was doing there. He said he couldn't be prevented from going to his bedroom whenever he wanted; anyway, he was on his way to fetch something. Put on my guard like this, I asked Frau K. whether there was a key to my bedroom, and next morning, on the second day, I locked myself in when I was getting dressed. Then, when I was going to lock myself in that afternoon, to rest on the sofa again, the key was missing. I am sure that Herr K. had removed it.'

So there we have the theme of being locked or not locked into the room, which first occurs in the dream, and to which another occasion happened to give a new role.[3]

Would what you said about *getting dressed quickly* have anything to do with those ideas?

'That was when I decided not to stay on with K. without Papa. On the following mornings I would have to fear being surprised by Herr K. while I was getting dressed, so I always *got dressed very quickly*. Papa was staying at his hotel, and Frau K. had always gone out early to go on an expedition with him. However, Herr K. did not pester me again.'

I understand that on the afternoon of the second day you decided to avoid such annoyance, and on the second, third, and fourth nights after the scene in the forest you had time to renew

---

[1] Compare the passage on p. 13, on doubts in remembering what was said.

[2] More memories have to come back to her before the question I put can be answered.

[3] I suspect, without saying so to Dora, that she picked up this element because of its symbolic significance. In German *Zimmer* [rooms] can often be taken to mean *Frauenzimmer* [females], and it cannot be all the same whether a female is open or closed. We also know what 'key' will open her.

that decision in your sleep. You already knew on the second afternoon, that is to say, before the dream, that you would not have the
key to allow you to lock yourself in while you were getting dressed
on the next morning—the third of your stay—so you could make
up your mind to get dressed as quickly as possible. However, your
dream came back every night because it corresponded to a *decision*. A decision remains just that until it is carried out. It is as if
you said to yourself: I shall not be able to rest, I shall not be able
to sleep properly until I am out of this house. Conversely, you say
in the dream: *As soon as I am out of the house I wake up.*

I will interrupt my record of the analysis here to assess this
fragmentary interpretation of a dream by the criteria of my general conclusions of the mechanism of the formation of dreams.
I explained in my book[1] that every dream was a wish represented
as if fulfilled, the representation was a disguise if the wish was a
repressed one, belonging to the unconscious, and except in the
dreams of children, only an unconscious wish or one bordering on
the unconscious has the power to create a dream. I believe I would
have found general agreement with this more certain if I had confined myself to saying that every dream has a sense that can be
found by a certain method of interpretation. Once the interpretation is complete, one can replace the dream by ideas that fit into
an easily recognizable place in conscious waking life. I could have
gone on to say that the meaning of the dream proves to be as complex as the dreamer's thought processes when awake. Sometimes
it is a desire granted, sometimes a fear realized, or perhaps a train
of thought continued in sleep, a decision (as in Dora's dream), an
intellectual reflection produced in sleep, and so on. Such a representation would have been easy to grasp, and could have supported itself on a whole series of well-interpreted examples such
as the dream analysed here.

Instead, I put forward a general claim confining the meaning of
dreams to a single form of thought, the representation of wishes,
and I aroused a general tendency to react by contradicting it.

---

[1] *The Interpretation of Dreams.*

However, I have to say that I did not think I had either the right or the duty to simplify a psychological process to make it more comfortable for readers, if that process confronted my investigation with a complication capable of resolution only elsewhere. It will therefore be especially valuable to me to show that apparent exceptions, such as this dream of Dora's, which at first looks like a decision made in the day and continued in sleep, in fact reinforce the controversial rule.

We still have a large part of the dream to interpret. I go on asking questions: What about the jewel-box that your Mama wants to retrieve?

'Mama loves jewellery, and Papa has given her a great deal of it.'

What about you?

'I used to love jewellery too, but I haven't worn it since I was ill.—Four years ago (a year before my dream) Papa and Mama had an angry quarrel over a piece of jewellery. Mama wanted a particular one, pearl drops to wear in her ears. But Papa doesn't like that kind of thing, and he gave her a bracelet instead of the earrings. She was furious, and told him that if he was going to spend so much money on a present that she didn't like, he might as well give it to someone else.'

And perhaps you thought you would like it?

'I don't know,[1] and I have no idea how Mama comes to be in the dream, when she wasn't with us in L.'[2]

I'll explain that to you later. Can't you think of anything else about the jewel-box? So far you've mentioned only Mama's jewellery, nothing about a box.

'Well, Herr K. gave me a valuable jewel-box as a present some time ago.'

So that was where the present given in return fits in. Perhaps you don't know that 'box of jewels' is a favourite term for the

---

[1] Her usual way at that time of acknowledging that she had repressed something.

[2] This remark, showing complete misunderstanding of the rules of dream-interpretation, which she otherwise knew well, as well as her hesitant manner, and the sparse yield of her ideas about the jewel-box, tell me that here we are dealing with material that has been very firmly repressed.

female genitals, the same thing as you hinted at not long ago when you mentioned your little purse.[1]

'I knew *you* were going to say that.'[2]

You mean that *you* knew the significance. The meaning of the dream is now becoming clearer. You said to yourself: that man is pursuing me, he wants to get into my room, danger threatens my box of jewels, and if something bad happens it will be Papa's fault. That is why you created a situation expressing the opposite in the dream: a danger from which Papa rescues you. In that region of the dream, moreover, everything becomes its opposite. You will soon hear why. However, the secret lies in your Mama. How does Mama come into it? As you know, she is your former rival in Papa's affections. Over that bracelet, you would have been happy to accept what Mama rejected. So now let us replace 'accept' by 'give', and 'rejected' by 'refused'. That means that you were ready to give Papa what Mama refuses him, and it was something to do with jewellery.[3] Now, remember the jewel-box that Herr K. gave you. You have there the beginning of a parallel chain of thought, in which Herr K. takes your Papa's place standing beside your bed. He has given you a jewel-box, so you are to give him your box of jewels. That is why I spoke just now of a present given in return. In that train of thought, your Mama's place will be taken by Frau K., who was certainly there at the time. So you are prepared to give Herr K. what his wife will not. Here we have the idea that must be repressed, with so much effort, making it necessary for you to turn all its elements into their opposite. As I have told you already about that dream, the dream confirms that you were reawakening your old love for Papa as a defence against your love for K. But what do all these efforts prove? Not only are you afraid of Herr K., you are even more afraid of yourself, of the temptation you feel to give way to him. You are thus confirming how intense your love for him was.[4]

[1] See below for this purse.

[2] A very usual way of fending off repressed knowledge that emerges from the unconscious.

[3] We shall also be able to find the interpretation of the ear-drops required by circumstances later.

[4] I add to this: And by the way, I must conclude, from the reappearance of the dream in the last few days, that you yourself think the same situation has recurred, and you have

Of course, she was unwilling to agree with this part of the interpretation.

However, I had thought of a further development of my theory of dream-interpretation, one that seemed indispensable both for the anamnesis of Dora's case and for my hypothesis about her dream. I promised to tell Dora what it was in our next session.

The fact is, I could not forget the hint that seemed to be given in the ambiguous phrases that I had noted (*there might be some mishap in the night, meaning that we had to go out*). To this was added the fact that the explanation of the dream seemed to me incomplete until a certain requirement was met. I do not say it is a general one, but I like to look for its presence. A normal dream stands, as it were, on two feet, one of which derives from the actual nature of the occasion for it, the other on a childhood event with serious consequences. The dream creates a link between the childhood experience and the present experience, it seeks to turn the present into a model of the dreamer's distant past. The wish that creates the dream always comes from childhood; it wants to bring childhood back to life again and again, to correct the present by reference to the childhood model. I thought that I could already detect the fragments that could be put together to allude to a childhood event in the content of this dream.

I began our discussion with a little experiment, which as usual succeeded. There happened to be a large box of matches on the table. I asked Dora to look around: did she see anything in particular on the table that was not usually there. She did not. Then I asked whether she knew why children are warned not to play with matches.

'Yes, because of the danger of fire. My uncle's children love playing with matches.'

That is not the only reason, I told her. They are warned not to play with fire, and there is a certain belief linked to that.

---

decided to withdraw from the course of treatment to which only your Papa brings you.—
The consequence showed how right my assumption was. My interpretation here comes
close to the subject of transference, which is extremely significant both practically and
theoretically, and I shall not find much more of an opportunity to go into it in this essay.

She didn't know what it was.—Well, people fear that they will wet the bed. That is probably based on the opposition of *water* and *fire*. Suppose they dream of fire and then try to put it out with water. I don't know just how to put this, but I can see that you find the opposition of water and fire in your dream very enlightening. Mama wants to save her jewel-box in case it *burns*, but in the dream the aim is to keep the jewel-box from getting *wet*. However, fire is not used only as the opposite of water; it also acts as the direct representation of love, of being in love, burnt by the fires of love. So from fire, one train of thought leads by way of this symbolic meaning to ideas of love, the other, after a connection of love with being wet has diverged in another direction, leads somewhere else by way of fire's opposite, water. Where does it lead? Think of the expressions you used: that there *might be an accident at night*, and it would mean you *had to go out*. Doesn't that indicate a physical need, and if you shift the mishap to childhood, can it mean anything but the risk of wetting the bed? And what do you do to prevent children from wetting the bed? You wake them up at night, *just as your Papa wakes you in the dream*, don't you? So that would be the real event which justifies your replacement of Herr K. waking you from sleep by substituting your Papa. I have to conclude that you suffered from bed-wetting longer than children usually do. It will have been the same with your brother. Your Papa says: *I don't want both my children . . .* to perish. Apart from that, your brother has nothing to do with the real situation involving K., he had not come to L. with you. What do your memories say about all this?

'I don't know about myself,' she replied, 'but my brother did wet the bed until he was six or seven, and he sometimes wet himself in the day as well.'

I was about to point out to her how much more easily she would remember such a thing about her brother than herself, when she went on with a memory that had come back to her. 'Yes, and so did I, but only for a while when I was seven or eight. It must have been bad, because now I remember that the doctor was asked for advice. It was just before my nervous asthma began.'

What did the doctor say?

'He said it was my weak nerves, and would pass off, and he prescribed a fortifying tonic.'[1]

I thought that we had now completed the interpretation of the dream.[2] Next day, however, she had something to add. She had forgotten, she said, that when she woke from the dream she always smelled smoke. The smoke suited the idea of fire, and also indicated that her dream had a special relationship to me, because whenever she had said there was nothing in something I suggested, I used to say: 'There's no smoke without fire.' She objected to this exclusively personal interpretation, however, by saying that both Herr K. and her Papa were passionately fond of smoking, and so indeed was I. She herself smoked beside the lake, and just before Herr K. began making his bungled advances to her he had rolled her a cigarette. She also thought she was sure that she remembered the smell of smoke had accompanied not only the last occurrence of the dream but also its three predecessors in L. As she would give no more information, it was left to me to fit this addition as I liked into the structure of the ideas behind the dream. As a starting-point I could use the fact that the smell of smoke had been a late memory to emerge, so it must have had to overcome particularly strong repression. That suggested that it probably belonged to the most veiled and best-repressed aspect of the dream, the temptation to show herself willing to do as a man wanted. It could hardly mean anything but a desire for a kiss, which given by a smoker would necessarily taste of smoke; however, there had been a kiss between the two of them about two years earlier, and it would certainly have been repeated more than once if the girl had yielded to the man's advances. Ideas of temptation thus seemed to refer back to the earlier scene, arousing the memory of the kiss, although as a girl who had sucked her thumb her disgust had protected her from its temptation at the time. Putting together these signs, which make a transference to me as

[1] This doctor was the only person she trusted, because this experience told her that he had not found out her secret. With anyone else, someone whose reactions she could not yet estimate, she felt anxiety in case he guessed the secret.

[2] The core of her dream, once translated, would run something like this: The temptation is so strong. Dear Papa, protect me again as you did when I was a child and you kept me from wetting the bed!

another smoker seem probable, I come to the view that one day it occurred to her, probably during our session, to wish that I would kiss her. That was the occasion for her warning dream to recur, and for her to make up her mind to break off the treatment. Looked at in that way, it all fits, but by virtue of the nature of the 'transference', it cannot be proved.

I can only hesitate between looking first at the findings of this dream for the case history, or dealing first with the objection to the dream theory. I decide on the former approach.

It is worth going thoroughly into the meaning of bed-wetting in the early history of neurotics. For the sake of clarity I will confine myself to emphasizing that in Dora's case the bed-wetting was out of the ordinary run. The trouble had not only exceeded the term considered normal for it, but from what she said had first died down and then came back relatively late, after her sixth year. To the best of my knowledge, there is no more likely cause of such bed-wetting than masturbation, which plays a part in the aetiology of bed-wetting that is still underestimated. In my experience, children themselves are very familiar with the connection, and all the psychological consequences derive from that fact as if they had never forgotten it. When Dora told me her dream we were following a line of research that led directly to such a confession of childhood masturbation. She had come up with the question, a little earlier, of why she was the one who fell ill, and before I could give any answer she laid the blame on her father. She founded this statement on knowledge, not ideas in the unconscious. To my surprise, the girl knew the nature of her father's illness. After he came back from consulting me, she had overheard a conversation in which his disorder was called by its name. Even earlier, at the time when he suffered from a detached retina, an eye-specialist called in for advice must have referred to its syphilitic aetiology, for at that time the curious and anxious girl overheard an old aunt telling her mother, 'He was ill even before you married,' adding something that Dora didn't understand, but later interpreted as having an indecent meaning.

So her father had contracted his illness because of his reckless way of life, and she assumed that she had inherited it from him.

I was careful not to tell her that, as mentioned above (note to p. 16), it is my own opinion that the offspring of syphilitics are particularly predisposed to severe neuropsychoses. This train of thought, blaming her father, continued on the unconscious level. For several days she showed small symptoms and characteristics through which she identified with her mother, which gave her an opportunity to indulge in the most impossible behaviour, and this suggested to me that she was thinking of going to stay in Franzensbad,* a resort that she and her mother had previously visited together—I don't remember what year that was in. Her mother suffered from pain in her lower body, and a discharge of matter like mucus that made it essential for her to take treatment in that resort. Dora's opinion—and again, that opinion was probably justified—was that this trouble was also caused by her Papa, who had transferred his venereal infection to her mother. Now that she had come to these conclusions, it was very understandable that, like a good many lay people, she classified gonorrhoea and syphilis, hereditary as well as caused by sexual intercourse, all together. Her persistent identification more or less obliged me to ask whether she had ever had a venereal infection herself, and now I discovered that she did in fact suffer from a discharge of *fluor albus* (leucorrhoea) herself, and could not remember when it had begun.

I now understood that the train of thought behind her vociferous accusations of her father concealed, as usual, self-blame, and I met her halfway by assuring her that, to my mind, a young girl's discharge of *fluor* indicates masturbation, and that compared to masturbation, all other causes of such an affliction retreat into the background.[1] She was therefore, I said, well on the way to answering her own question—why she had fallen ill—if she admitted to masturbation, probably in her childhood years. She firmly denied being able to remember any such thing. But a few days later she brought up a subject that I had to assume brought us closer to such an admission. She was wearing around her neck that day, as I never saw her do before or afterwards, a little drawstring purse

---

[1] (Added in 1923.) An extreme opinion which I would no longer hold today.

in a very modern style, and was playing with it as she lay talking to me by opening it, inserting a finger, closing it again, and so on. I watched her for a while, and then told her what a *symptomatic action* is. Symptomatic actions are my name for those ways in which someone will perform an action automatically—as we say, unconsciously—without paying any attention to it, and as if in play, and then if asked about it denies that it has any particular significance, saying that it is a trivial matter, mere chance. But closer observation shows that such actions, which the conscious mind does not or does not want to acknowledge, express unconscious ideas and impulses, and thus are valuable and instructive in that they allow the unconscious to find expression. There are two kinds of conscious reactions to symptomatic actions. If they can be unobtrusively motivated, people will notice what they are doing; if there is no such excuse present in the conscious mind, then as a rule they will not notice that they are carrying them out at all. In Dora's case it was easy to find motivation: 'Why shouldn't I wear a little purse like this now that it's the latest fashion?' But such a justification does not make it impossible to find the unconscious origin of whatever the action is. On the other hand, that origin, and the significance to be ascribed to the action, cannot be conclusively shown. We have to be content with establishing that such a significance fits extremely well, in the context of the present situation, into the agenda of the unconscious mind.

On another occasion I will present a collection of such symptomatic actions as they can be observed in both healthy and nervous people. Interpretation is sometimes very easy. Dora's little purse, which was in two parts, was a representation of her genitals, and the way she played with it, opening it and putting a finger inside it, an uninhibited but unmistakable mime of how she would like to masturbate them. Recently I came upon a similar and very amusing case. An elderly lady takes out a little bone box in the middle of a sitting, allegedly to moisten her mouth with a sweet, tries to open it, and then hands it to me, so that I can see for myself how hard it is to open. I express my suspicion that this box must have some special meaning; this is the first time I have seen it, although its owner has been visiting me for consultations for over a year.

To this the lady says excitedly, 'I always have this box with me. I take it everywhere I go!' She calms down only when, smiling, I point out how well her remarks fit another meaning. The box*—πύξις—like Dora's little purse, is only another representation of the shell of Venus,* the female genitals!

There is a great deal of such symbolism in life, and we usually pass it by without a thought. When I set myself the task of casting light on what people hide—not under compulsion, by hypnosis, but from what they say and their behaviour—I thought it would be more difficult than it really is. Those who have eyes to see and ears to hear will soon convince themselves that mortals cannot hide any secret. If our lips are sealed we talk volubly with our fingertips; we betray ourselves through every pore. And so the task of uncovering ideas, however deeply hidden, is perfectly capable of resolution.

Dora's symbolic action involving the purse did not immediately precede her dream. She ushered in the session that brought us the story of her dream with another symptomatic action. When I entered the room where she was waiting, she quickly hid a letter that she had been reading. I naturally asked who her letter was from, and at first she did not want to tell me. Then information came out that was of no interest in itself, and had no connection with my treatment. It was a letter from her grandmother, saying that she wished she would write more often. I think that she merely wanted to 'pretend' there was a secret, hinting that her doctor was about to make her tell her real secret. I now explain her disinclination to see any new doctor by her fear that he would get to the root of her disorder, during examination (noticing her leucorrhoea) or in asking her questions (finding out about her bed-wetting), and would work out that the cause was masturbation. She was always very disparaging in what she said about doctors, whom she had obviously overestimated in the past.

Complaints that her father had made her ill, hiding blame for herself—the leucorrhoea—playing with the little purse—bed-wetting after her sixth year—a secret that she does not want the doctors to find out: I consider that all these indications provided me with proof positive of childhood masturbation. In her case

I had begun to suspect the masturbation when she told me about her cousin's stomach-cramps (see pp. 31–2), and then identified with that cousin by complaining of suffering from the same painful sensations for days on end. The frequency with which stomach-pains occur in women who masturbate is well known. According to a personal communication to me from W. Fliess,* it is exactly such instances of gastralgia that can be cured by applying cocaine to the 'gastric spot' that he has found in the nose, and then cauterizing it. Dora consciously confirmed that she had often suffered stomach-pains herself, and had good reasons for thinking that her cousin masturbated. It is very usual for the sick to recognize a connection in others that they cannot see in themselves because of feelings of resistance. And she was no longer denying it, although she said she could still remember nothing. I also consider the timing of her bed-wetting to 'just before I developed nervous asthma' clinically useful. Hysterical symptoms almost never occur while children are still masturbating, only in periods of abstinence;[1] they express a substitute for masturbatory satisfaction, for which a desire is preserved in the unconscious as long as there is no other kind of more normal satisfaction, where that is still possible. The latter condition is the turning-point at which a possible cure for hysteria can be provided by marriage and normal sexual intercourse. If satisfaction in marriage is then withheld again, for instance by *coitus interruptus*, alienation from the marriage partner, and so forth, then the libido seeks out the old riverbed where it once flowed, and expresses itself again in hysterical symptoms.

I wish I could say for certain when and by what particular influence Dora's masturbation was repressed, but as the analysis was never completed I cannot offer anything but fragmentary material here. We have heard that she was wetting the bed until near the time of her first episode of dyspnoea. The only thing she was able to say in explanation was that at the time her Papa had gone away for the good of his health for the first time. This scrap of memory that she retained must hint at a relationship to the aetiology of

[1] The same is true in principle of adults, but here even relative abstinence, restraining masturbation, is enough, in those with a strong libido, to allow hysteria and masturbation to occur together.

her dyspnoea. Symptomatic actions and other signs gave me good grounds to assume that the child, whose bedroom was next to her parents' room, eavesdropped when her father was making love to his wife one night, and heard his gasping breath during coitus— he was a man who suffered from breathlessness anyway. In such cases, children guess at the sexual element in these strange sounds. The means of expressing sexual arousal are already latent in them as inborn mechanisms. Years ago, I explained how dyspnoea and the thudding heartbeat of hysteria and anxiety neurosis are only fragments of the act of coitus that have become detached from it, and in many cases, like Dora's, I could trace the symptom of dyspnoea and her nervous asthma back to the same cause, overhearing adults engaged in sexual intercourse. Under the influence of sympathetic feeling setting in at that time, a change in the child's sexuality can easily occur, replacing a tendency towards masturbation by one of anxiety. A little while later, when her father was away and his child, who was in love with him, thought of him with longing, the impression was repeated as an attack of asthma. From what she remembered of the causes of this attack, we can guess at the anxious train of thought accompanying it. She first had asthma when she had overexerted herself on a climbing expedition, and could have felt genuine breathlessness. In addition, it will have occurred to her that her father was forbidden to go climbing and must not overstrain himself because his breath came short, and then came the memory of his exertions with Mama in the night— might they not have harmed him?—then concern for herself, and whether she had not overexerted herself in masturbation leading to sexual orgasm with dyspnoea, and then the return of that dyspnoea, now reinforced, as a symptom. I could deduce part of this chain of events from the analysis; the rest I had to complete for myself. We have seen that, once masturbation is diagnosed, the material for a subject can be put together only in fragments gleaned from different times and different circumstances.[1]

[1] The evidence for infantile masturbation is similarly obtained in other cases. The material for it is usually of much the same nature: indications of *fluor albus* (leucorrhoea), bed-wetting, ceremonial cleansing of the hands (compulsive hand-washing), and so on. We can always deduce for certain from the symptoms of a case whether the habit was

A series of very important questions on the aetiology of hysteria now arise: can Dora's case be regarded as typical, is it the only type of cause for it, and so on. I am certainly right in saying that they must wait to be answered until a wider range of similar cases have been analysed. I would also have to begin by adjusting the position from which the question is asked. Instead of saying Yes or No to whether the aetiology of such cases is to be sought in childhood masturbation, I would first have to explore the concept of aetiology in psychoneuroses. The viewpoint from which I could provide answers would turn out to be some way from the viewpoint of those asking me questions. It will suffice in this case if we can say for certain that infantile masturbation can be proved, that it cannot be a chance factor or of no significance for the clinical picture.[1] We shall get further understanding of Dora's symptoms if we look at the significance of her admission that she had a discharge of *fluor albus*. She had learned to describe the disorder of leucorrhoea as 'catarrh' when a similar infection made it necessary for her mother to go to Franzensbad, and the word acted as a

found out by someone looking after a child or not, whether the child has been weaned off the habit, or has had a sudden change of mind and then desisted from this form of sexual activity. Dora's masturbation remained undiscovered, but came to a sudden end (fear of doctors who might find out her secret, replacement by dyspnoea). Patients regularly dispute the evidence of such indications, even when a discharge or a maternal warning ('that will make you stupid; it's poisonous') lingers in the memory. Some time later, however, the long-repressed memory of this episode of childhood sexuality is certain to surface again in all cases.—In a patient with compulsions which were directly derived from infantile masturbation, such features as forbidding herself to do something, punishing herself for it—if she had done one thing, then she mustn't do another—taking care not to be disturbed, making sure there is an interval between doing one thing (with her hands) and another, hand-washing, and so on prove to derive directly from the efforts of someone looking after her to wean her off her habit. The warning that it is disgusting and harmful is all that regularly remains in the memory. See on this subject my *Three Essays on the Theory of Sexuality*.

[1] Her habit of masturbation must be linked in some way to her brother, for in this connection she said, with emphasis showing its nature as a screen memory, that her brother regularly passed on all the childhood infections to her; he did not suffer much from them, but she did. Her brother is also prevented from 'perishing' in the dream; he also suffered from bed-wetting, but stopped before his sister. In a way it was another screen memory when she said that she had kept pace with her brother in her studies until her first illness, but from then on lagged behind him—as if up to that point she had been a boy, and only then became girlish. She had been wild, but after her first attack of asthma calmed down and was well behaved. In her mind that illness marked the boundary between two phases of sexual life, the first one male and the second female in nature.

means of gaining access, by way of their expression in the symptom of coughing, to a whole range of ideas about her Papa's responsibility for the disorder. Her cough, which must have been the result of a mild attack of real nasal catarrh, was in any case an imitation of her father's lung trouble and enabled her to express her pity and concern for him. In addition, however, it was her way of proclaiming to the world, so to speak, something of which she had not yet become consciously aware: 'I am Papa's daughter. I have catarrh, like him. He had made me ill just as he made Mama ill. I inherit from him the wicked passions that are punished by illness.'[1]

We can now try putting together the various determining factors that we have found for Dora's attacks of coughing and hoarseness. Lowest in level is a real, organic tickle in the throat causing her to cough, the grain of sand around which the oyster forms the pearl. We can pinpoint the location of this sensation because it concerns a part of the body which has retained its importance as an erogenous zone to the girl to a high degree. It is therefore suitable to express the stimulated libido, fixed by what is probably the first psychological layer, sympathetic imitation of her sick father, and then by blaming herself for her 'catarrh'. The same group of symptoms is also capable of representing her relationship to Herr K., along with her regrets of his absence, and of expressing a wish to be a better wife to him than Frau K. When part of her libido turns to her father again, the symptom acquires perhaps its final significance as a representation of sexual intercourse with her father by identifying with Frau K. I would guarantee that this sequence is by no means complete. Unfortunately, the incomplete analysis is unable to follow the change of meaning temporally,

---

[1] The word 'catarrh' played the same part in the case history of the fourteen-year-old girl that I have summarized in a few lines on pp. 19–20, note. I had installed the child in a boarding-house with an intelligent lady who acted as a nurse for me. This lady told me that her small patient could not bear her presence while she was going to bed, and that in bed at night she coughed a great deal, although not at all in the daytime. When she was asked about this symptom, all the girl could think of was that her grandmother, who was said to have catarrh, coughed like that. Then it was clear that she too had 'catarrh', and did not want to have any witness to her careful cleansing of herself in the evening. The discharge of mucus, thus shifted from lower to higher in the body by the use of the word catarrh, was even of unusual intensity.

showing the sequence of events and the coexistence of various meanings. We could expect a complete analysis to answer these demands.

I must not omit to go into further connections of Dora's genital catarrh, or leucorrhoea, and her hysterical symptoms. In times when psychological explanation of hysteria was still far in the future, I used to hear older, experienced colleagues claim that in hysterical women with *fluor albus* worsening of that disorder regularly led to an intensification of their hysteria, particularly loss of appetite and a tendency to vomit. No one was really sure what the connection was, but I think they were inclined to accept the view of gynaecologists, who are known to assume that the direct, organically disruptive influence of genital infections acts widely on the nervous functions, although usually not much evidence to that effect can be found. In our present state of knowledge, indeed, we cannot exclude such a direct, organic factor, but at least it is easier to show the psychological way in which it is expressed. Pride in the appearance of their genitalia is a considerable part of women's vanity; infections in that area thought likely to provoke dislike or even disgust are felt to be extraordinarily injurious to that pride and their self-esteem, making women irritable, sensitive, and suspicious. Abnormal secretions from the mucous membrane of the vagina are regarded as disgusting.

Let us remind ourselves that when Herr K. had kissed her, Dora felt a lively sensation of disgust, and that we found reasons to complement her tale of this scene of kissing by assuming that she felt his erect penis pressing against her while she was in his embrace. We now discover, in addition, that the same governess whom she rejected for disloyalty had told Dora, from her own experience, that all men were light-minded and unreliable. To Dora, that would have meant that all men were like her Papa. And she thought that her father had venereal disease, having infected her and her mother with it. She could therefore imagine that all men had venereal disease, and her concept of that term was of course formed by reference to her one personal experience. To have venereal disease, then, meant to have a disgusting discharge—was this another reason for the disgust she felt at the moment

when K. embraced her? Transferring that disgust to the man's
touch, then, would have been projected back on him by the primi-
tive mechanism mentioned above (see p. 29), ultimately relating
to her own discharge.

I suspect that we have here an unconscious chain of ideas cast
over preformed organic connections rather like festoons of flower
over a metal frame, so that at another time different ideas can be
traced between the first idea and its conclusion. However, knowledge of the detailed connections that took effect is of irreplaceable
value in resolving the symptoms. It is only because the analysis
was broken off, unfinished, that we have to resort to assumptions
to fill the gaps in Dora's case. What I shall now suggest to fill those
gaps leans entirely on other cases that were subject to thorough
analysis.

The dream through the analysis of which we have gained the preceding conclusions corresponds, as we found out, to a resolution
of Dora's taken as she falls asleep. It therefore recurs every night
until she has carried out that resolution, and reappears years later
as soon as there is an occasion to take an analogous resolution. The
resolution can be consciously put into words something like this:
I must get away from this house where, as I have seen, my virginity is in danger, I will go away with Papa, and when I am getting
up in the morning I will be careful not to be taken by surprise.
These ideas find clear expression in the dream; they belong to a
current that has come to dominate the conscious mind in waking
life. We can guess at a more darkly presented train of thought
behind them, corresponding to the opposite current, so that it has
been repressed. It culminates in the temptation to give herself
to the man in gratitude for the love and affection he has shown
her over recent years, perhaps reviving her memory of the only
kiss she has so far received from him. But according to the theory
I developed in my *Interpretation of Dreams*, such elements are not
enough to form a dream. A dream is not a resolution to be carried
out, but a wish shown as fulfilled, perhaps a wish from the dreamer's childhood. We have an obligation to see whether this idea is
not refuted by the dream.

The dream does in fact contain childish material which, at first glance, stands in reasonable relation to the resolution of leaving Herr K.'s house and the temptation she felt there. Why do the memories of childhood bed-wetting and the trouble her father took to keep her clean as a child surface? We can reply, because it is possible to repress intense ideas of temptation only with the help of this train of thought, making her resolution to oppose those ideas dominant. The child decides to flee *with* her father; in reality she is fleeing *to* her father in fear of the man pursuing her; she revives a childhood love of her father to protect her from her recent love for a stranger. Her father is himself in part to blame for her present danger, having left her at the mercy of the stranger because of a love-interest of his own. How much better it was when that same father loved no one more than her, and went to the trouble of saving her from the dangers that threatened her then! Her infantile and now unconscious wish to place her father in the position of the stranger has the potential to form a dream. If there has been a situation that differed from the present one only in the person represented, this becomes the main situation in the content of the dream. And there is indeed such a situation; like Herr K. the previous day, her father once stood beside her bed, and perhaps woke her with a kiss, as maybe Herr K. had intended to do. Her resolution to flee from the house is therefore unable to form a dream in itself; it becomes able to do so when accompanied by another resolution supported by childhood wishes. Her wish to replace Herr K. by her father gives the dream its driving force. I am reminded of the interpretation obliging me to see her intensified train of thought relating to her father's relationship with Frau K. as the revival of an infantile love for her father in order to keep her repressed love for Herr K. still in a state of repression; this change in my patient's mental life is mirrored in the dream.

I have set down some remarks about the relationship between waking thought continued in sleep—the remnants of the day—and the unconscious wishes that form dreams in the *Interpretation of Dreams*, and I will quote them here unchanged, since I have nothing to add to them, and analysis of this dream of Dora's supports my theory of the process.

'I will admit that there is an entire class of dreams *stimulated* principally or even exclusively by the remnants of daily life, and I think that my wish to be called *professor extraordinarius* some day[1] would have allowed me to sleep peacefully that night but for my anxiety about my friend's health, which was still on my mind from the day before. But that anxiety would not have been enough to create a dream; the *stimulus* that the dream required had to be supplied by a wish. It was the task of my anxiety to create such a wish as the motivating force behind the dream. To put it metaphorically, it is perfectly possible for a daytime idea to play the part of an *entrepreneur* supplying the dream, but the entrepreneur who, as we say, has the idea and the motive to carry it out can do nothing without capital; he needs a *capitalist* who will meet the expense, and that capitalist, who meets the psychological expense of the dream, is always, and inevitably, whatever the waking thought from the day may be, a *wish from the unconscious.*'

Anyone who has learnt to appreciate the fine structure of such mental products as dreams will not be surprised to find that Dora's wish for her father to replace the man trying to tempt her revived memories, not of random material from childhood, but of material germane to the most intimate reasons for repressing temptation. For if Dora felt unable to succumb to her love for the man, if it was not expressed but repressed, then that decision was closely connected with her precocious sexual pleasure and its consequences, bed-wetting, mucous discharge, and disgust. Depending on the accumulated effect of the constitutional conditions, a past history of that kind can be the foundation for two kinds of reaction to the demands made by love: either full and unresisting abandonment to sexuality verging on perversion, or rejection of it accompanied by neurotic illness. In the case of my patient, her constitution, and the level of her intellectual and moral education, had brought her to decide on the second alternative.

I would like to emphasize, in particular, that analysis of this dream has given us access to details of the most pathogenically effective experiences, those that were not otherwise accessible to

---

[1] This refers to the analysis of the dream there taken as a pattern.

memory, or at least to reproduction of it. The memory of Dora's childhood bed-wetting, as it turns out, had already been repressed. Dora had never mentioned the details of Herr K.'s advances to her; the connection had not occurred to her.

I will add a few more remarks about the synthesis of this dream. Its dream-work begins on the afternoon of the second day after the scene in the forest, when Dora notices that she can no longer lock the door of her room. She says to herself: I am threatened by serious danger, and resolves not to be on her own in the house, but to leave when her Papa does. This resolution becomes capable of creating a dream because it can continue in the unconscious mind. There, the fact that she can call on her childhood love of her father to protect her against present temptation corresponds to it. The change taking place in her mind becomes fixated and brings her to the viewpoint that represents her supervalent train of thought (jealousy of Frau K. over her father, as if she were in love with him herself). A struggle goes on inside her between the temptation to give in to the man making advances, and the sum of her resistance to it. The motives for the latter consist of considerations of proper behaviour and circumspection, hostility as a result of the governess's revelation (jealousy, wounded pride; see below), and a neurotic element, her present rejection of sex, which is based on her childhood history.

The dream changes the resolution buried deep in her unconscious mind, to flee to her father, into a situation where the wish for her father to save her from danger is granted. However, there is another idea in the way of the change, and it has to be removed: it is her father himself who has put her in that danger. We shall find that the repressed hostile emotion felt for her father here (a wish for revenge) is one of the driving forces behind the second dream.

Following the conditions of dream formation, the imagined situation is chosen so as to repeat an infantile experience. It is a particular triumph for it to succeed in turning a recent situation, for instance, the occasion for the dream, into an infantile one, and here that is achieved by the purely coincidental nature of the material. Her father often stood beside her bed and woke her when she was a child, just as Herr K. has done now. The change in Dora's mind is cogently symbolized by her substitution of her father for Herr K. in this situation.

However, in the past her father woke her to keep her from wetting the bed.

This wetness is a determining factor in the further content of the dream, in which, however, it is represented only by a distant allusion and by its opposite.

The opposite of 'wet' and 'water' can easily be seen as 'fire' and 'burning'. The coincidental fact that her father, on arriving at the resort of L., expressed fear of the danger of fire helps her decision to make the danger from which her father saves her into a fire. The situation chosen for the dream image depends on that coincidence and the opposite of 'wet': there is a fire, her father stands beside her bed to wake her. His chance remark would probably not have that meaning in the dream if it did not go so well with the victorious counter-current of her mind, her wish to see her father helping and rescuing her. He guessed at the danger as soon as he arrived, he was right! (In reality, it was he who put the girl in that danger.)

In the ideas of the dream, the 'wetness', as a result of easily established connections, assumes the role of a nodal point for several circles of thought. The idea of 'wet' does not belong solely with bed-wetting, but also with the ideas circling around sexual temptation which, in repressed form, stand behind the content of this dream. She knows that wetness is a part of sexual intercourse, that during copulation the man transfers something fluid to the woman, in the form of *drops*. She knows that danger resides exactly there, that she faces the task of keeping her genitals from getting wet.

At the same time, another circle of associations joins the ideas of 'wet' and 'drops', the idea of the disgusting discharge that in her more mature years probably makes her feel ashamed, just as bed-wetting did when she was a child. Here 'wet' means the same as 'polluted'. Her genitals, which are supposed to be kept clean, have been polluted by the discharge of mucus suffered by her mother as well as herself (pp. 69–70). She seems to understand that her Mama's obsession with cleanliness is the reaction to this pollution.

Both circles then meet to form one: Mama was given both sexual wetness and the polluting *fluor* by Papa. Her jealousy of Mama is inseparable from the circle of thoughts summoning up her infantile love of her father to protect her. But that material cannot yet be represented. However, if a memory can be found that relates equally well to both circles of thought associated with 'wet', but avoids being disgusting, it will be able to take on the function of representation in the content of the dream.

There is such a memory in the idea of the 'pearl drop' earrings that Mama had wanted as an item of jewellery. Apparently linking this reminiscence to both circles—sexual wetness and pollution— is an outer, superficial one conveyed by the words, for 'drop' is a word capable of more than one meaning, and 'jewellery' signifies purity as a rather strained opposite to the impurity of pollution. In reality, we can trace very firmly established associations of content. The memory derives from Dora's jealousy of her Mama, beginning in infancy but well developed. All the meaning attached to the ideas of sexual intercourse between her parents, the affliction of leucorrhea, and her Mama's obsessive passion for cleaning can be conveyed over those two verbal bridges.

However, yet another displacement in the content of the dream must jostle for position. Not the idea of 'drops', which are closer to the original idea of 'wet', but the more remotely associated 'jewellery' is accepted into the dream. It could thus have meant, when this element was fitted into the already fixated dream structure: Mama wants to save her jewellery. In the new version, as 'jewel-box', the influence of elements from the underlying circle of ideas involving temptation by Herr K. makes itself felt. Herr K. has not given Dora jewellery, but he did give her a little box, representing all the attention and affection that she is now supposed to be grateful for. And the combination that now appears, 'jewel-box', has another particular value. Is 'jewel-box' not a common image for the unstained, intact female genitalia? And in another aspect it is a harmless term, and thus highly suitable both to indicate and conceal the sexual ideas behind the dream.

So we have 'Mama's jewel-box' in two places in the content of the dream, and this element replaces the mention of infantile jealousy, the drops for her ears, that is to say, sexual wetness, pollution by *fluor*, and on the other hand present ideas of temptation that call for love to be returned and present a picture of the imminent sexual situation, which is both desired and threatening. The 'jewel-box' element is the striking outcome of intensification and displacement, and a compromise between currents flowing in opposite directions. Its double appearance in the dream content probably points to the complex nature of its sources, both infantile and in the present.

The dream is the reaction to a fresh and exciting experience which must inevitably awaken Dora's memory of her only other and earlier analogous experience. That is the scene when Herr K. kissed her in his shop, and she reacted with disgust. The same scene, however, can be reached by way of other associations, by the circle of ideas involving 'catarrh' or discharge (see p. 70) and by her present temptation. It makes its own contribution to the content of the dream, which has to suit the imagined situation. Something is burning . . . the kiss probably did taste of smoke, so she smells smoke in the dream that here continues after waking.

In the analysis of this dream I unfortunately and carelessly left a gap. The remark: *I do not want both my children to perish* (and we can probably add, drawing on ideas in the dream: of the consequences of masturbation) is attributed to the father. Such dream dialogue is regularly put together from scraps of real, waking speech, either remembered or overheard. I ought to have inquired further about the real origin of this remark. An answer to that question might have shown the structure of the dream as more involved but also, certainly, easier to recognize.

Are we to think that this dream had exactly the same content back in L. as when it recurred during Dora's cure? Not necessarily, I think. Experience shows that people often think they have had the same dream, but the various appearances of the recurrent dream differ in many details and have other wide-ranging variations. For instance, one of my patients says that she had her favourite dream today: it always recurs in the same way: she is swimming in the blue sea, enjoying the sensation of cutting a path through the waves, and so on. Closer investigation shows that now one and now another detail is added to the common background of all occurrences of it: for instance, on one occasion she is swimming in the sea while it is frozen, among icebergs. Other dreams, that she herself does not try to claim are the same, show that they are closely related to this recurrent one. For instance, she sees the highlands and low-lying plains of Helgoland at the same time and in their real dimensions (she saw them in a photograph), there is a ship on the sea in which two of her youthful acquaintances are travelling, and so on.

It is certain that Dora's dream, recurring during her treatment—perhaps without changing its manifest content—had gained new meaning relevant to the present. In its dream ideas it included a reference to my treatment, and corresponded to her renewed resolution to keep out of danger. If her memory did not deceive her when she claimed to have already smelt smoke after waking back in L., we must recognize that she very neatly fitted my comment, 'There's no smoke without fire,' into the pre-existing form of the dream, where it seems to be used in over-determination of the last element. It was undeniably chance that brought her the final actual occasion for the dream, her mother's locking of the dining-room, which meant that her brother was confined to his bedroom, an allusion to Herr K.'s advances to Dora in L., where her resolution matured on finding that she could not lock her bedroom door. Perhaps her brother did not feature in her dreams at the earlier time, so that her father's remark about 'both my children' reached the content of the dream only after this last occasion for it.

III

THE SECOND DREAM

A FEW weeks after her first dream, Dora had her second dream, and when I had dealt with that the analysis was broken off. This dream cannot be made quite so transparent as the first, but it provided welcome confirmation of an assumption that had become necessary about my patient's mental state, filled in a gap in her memory, and allowed deep insight into the origin of another of her symptoms.

Dora said: *I am walking in a town I don't know, and I see streets and squares that are strange to me.*[1] *Then I reach a house where I am living, I go to my room and find a letter from Mama there. As I have left home without my parents' knowledge, says her letter, she did not want to write and tell me that Papa was ill. Now he has died, and, she writes, if you like*[2] *you can come home. I start out for the station and ask about 100 times: where is the station? I am always told: another five minutes' walk away. Then I see a dense forest ahead of me, I go into it, and there I ask a man whom I meet. He tells me: the station is another 2½ hours' walk away.*[3] *He offers to accompany me. I decline the offer, and go on alone. I see the station ahead of me, but I cannot reach it. And I have the usual feeling of anxiety you get in a dream when you are making no progress. Then I am at home; I must have travelled by train in between, but I don't know anything about that.—I go into the porter's lodge, and ask the porter where our apartment is. The maid opens the door to me, and says: Your Mama and the others have already gone to the cemetery.*[4]

There was some difficulty in interpreting this dream. As a result of the curious circumstances, connected with its content, in

---

[1] Here there was an important addition: *In one of the squares I see a monument.*

[2] Here came the addition: *After that word there was a question-mark: if you like?*

[3] She repeats, a second time: *2 hours.*

[4] In our next session she made two additions to this: *I see myself particularly clearly going up the stairs*, and: *After her answer I go into my room, but not feeling at all sad, and read from a large book that is lying on my desk.*

which we broke off the analysis, not everything had been explained, and in addition there is the fact that my memory has not preserved the sequence of her revelations entirely reliably throughout. I will begin by mentioning the theme that the analysis was following when the dream intervened. For some time, Dora herself had been asking questions about the connection between her actions and the motives that could be ascribed to them. One of these questions was: why did I say nothing about that scene by the lake the first day after it? Her second was: why did I then suddenly tell my parents? I thought that we still needed an adequate explanation of why she felt so insulted by Herr K.'s advances, particularly as I was beginning to see that to Herr K. himself, his advances to Dora had not been an idle attempt at seduction. I interpreted her telling her parents about the incident at all as an action that was already influenced by a morbid desire for revenge. I would expect a normal girl to get over such things by her own efforts.

I shall therefore present the material available to me for the analysis of this dream in the rather random order of my memory of it.

She is walking alone in a strange town and sees streets and squares. She assures me that it was certainly not B., which had been my first guess, but a town where she had never been. It seemed obvious to say: then you could have seen pictures or photographs from which you take the images of the dream. After this remark came the addition to what she had already said, the mention of the monument in a square, and then she immediately knew the source of it. At Christmas she had been given an album with views of the sights in a German spa resort, and she had been looking for it only the day before her dream, to show it to the relations who were staying with her family. It was in a box of pictures that she could not find at once, and she asked her Mama: *Where is the box?*[1] One of the pictures showed a square with a monument in it. The donor of the album was a young engineer with whom she had once been briefly acquainted in the manufacturing town. The young man

[1] In the dream she asks: *Where is the station?* I drew a conclusion from this similarity of phrasing that I will develop later.

had taken a post in Germany so as to make himself independent as soon as he could, but he used every opportunity to remind her of him, and it was easy to guess that when his position had improved he was planning to approach Dora and ask her to marry him. But that would take time, so he had to wait.

The idea of wandering around a strange town was over-determined. It led to one of the waking reasons for it. A young cousin had come to visit Dora's family for the holiday, and she was to show him the sights of Vienna. This reason for the dream incident was insignificant in itself. However, her cousin reminded her of her first brief visit to Dresden. At that time she walked around the city, which was new to her, and naturally did not fail to visit the famous picture gallery. Another cousin, who was in her party and knew Dresden, offered to act as a guide to the gallery. *But she declined his offer and went on alone*, stopping in front of the pictures she liked. She spent *two hours* in quiet, dreamy admiration of Raphael's *Sistine Madonna*. When she was asked what she liked so much about the picture, she was at a loss for a clear answer. At last she simply said: the Madonna.

It is certain that these ideas really do belong to the material from which her dream was formed. They include elements that we find again unchanged in the content of the dream (she declines the offer of a man's company and goes on alone—there is a wait of two hours). I have already noticed that 'pictures' are a nodal point in the fabric of the dream ideas (the pictures in the album—the pictures in Dresden). I would also like to pick out the theme of the Madonna, the virginal mother, for further investigation. Above all, however, I see that she is identifying with a young man in this first part of the dream. He is wandering around in a strange place, trying to reach a destination, but he is held up, he needs patience, he must wait. If she was thinking of the engineer, it would have meant that his aim was to get possession of a woman, herself. Instead, however, he is looking for a station. However, judging by the relation between the question in the dream and the question really asked, we may substitute a *box*. A box and a woman go better together.

She asks about a hundred times . . . This leads to another and less insignificant cause of the dream. The evening before she had it, after a party, her father asked her to fetch him the bottle of cognac; he could never sleep without a nightcap of cognac. She asked her mother for the key to the larder, but her mother was deep in conversation and did not answer until Dora snapped at her impatiently: I've asked you about a *hundred times* where the key is. In reality, of course, she had asked her question only about *five times*.[1]

Where is the key? sounds to me like the male counterpart to the question: Where is the box? (see the first dream, p. 56). These are questions about the genitals.

In the same party of relations someone drank a toast to Dora's Papa, expressing a hope that he would continue in good health for a long time, and so forth. At that her father's tired face had twitched in an odd way, and she had understood the thoughts he must be suppressing. Poor sick man that he was—who knew how long a life lay before him?

Here we come to the *content of the letter* in the dream. Her father had died, she had left home of her own accord. In connection with the letter in the dream, I reminded her of the farewell letter that she had written her parents, or that she had at least left lying around where they could see it. That letter was intended to frighten her Papa and induce him to break off his relationship with Frau K., or at least to be revenged on him if he could not be persuaded to do that. We come to the subject of her death and the death of her father (a *cemetery* is mentioned later in the dream). Would it be wrong to assume that the situation forming the façade of the dream corresponds to a fantasy of revenge on her father? Her sympathetic thoughts of him the day before would suit that idea. However, the fantasy was that she would go away from home to a strange place, and her father's heart would break out of grief and longing for her. Then she would be revenged. She knew very well what her father was missing if he couldn't sleep now without cognac.[2]

---

[1] In the content of the dream the number five stands for the length of time to reach the station: 5 minutes. In my book about the *Interpretation of Dreams* I have shown, citing many examples, how to deal with numbers occurring in thoughts in the dream. They are usually found to have been torn out of their old context and relocated in a new one.

[2] Sexual satisfaction is undoubtedly the best soporific, just as insomnia is generally the result of frustration. Her father could not sleep because he was missing intercourse with the woman he loved. Cf. the remark below: 'I get no satisfaction from my wife.'

We will make a note of the *desire for revenge* as a new element for a later synthesis of the dream ideas.

However, the content of the letter had to allow further determination. Where did the addition of 'if you like' come from?

Here she remembered the question-mark added after the word 'like', and recognized the words as a quotation from a letter from Frau K. containing the invitation to L., the lakeside resort. In this letter, after the interpolated words 'if you like?' there was a question-mark that looked very striking in the middle of the structure of the sentence.

So that brought us back to the scene beside the lake and the puzzles connected with it. I asked her to describe the scene to me again, in detail. At first little that was new could be gleaned from it. Herr K. had begun on a fairly serious speech, but she did not let him finish it. As soon as she understood what it was all about she slapped his face and ran away. I wanted to know what words he had used; she remembers only his justification: 'You know I get no satisfaction from my wife.'[1] She then decided to walk around the lake back to L., so as to avoid his company, and *asked a man whom she met how far she still had to go*. When he said, 'For another 2½ hours', she gave up that idea, and went in search of the boat that was leaving soon afterwards. Herr K. was there again and approached her, asked her to forgive him and say nothing about the incident. But she did not reply.—Yes, the *forest* in the dream was very like the forest on the banks of the lake where the scene that she had just described for the second time took place. And she had seen the same dense forest yesterday in a painting in the exhibition at the Secession building. And there were *nymphs* to be seen in the background of the picture.[2]

Now my suspicion became a certainty. The words *Bahnhof* (station)[3] and *Friedhof* (cemetery) in the place of the female genitalia were striking enough, but had attracted my close attention to

---

[1] These words will lead to the solution of one of our puzzles.

[2] Here for the third time we had the word *Bild*, picture, in the context of *Städtebilder*, cityscapes, and the Dresden picture gallery, but in a much more significant connection. Through what the picture shows the *Bild* becomes a *Weibsbild*, a woman, with the connotations of a forest and nymphs.

[3] The 'station' moreover serves 'traffic/intercourse'.

another word formed with the same suffix of -*hof*, the *Vorhof*, a forecourt, but also the term for the genital atrium, a specific part of the genitalia. That could have been just an amusing coincidental mistake, but now that we had 'nymphs' in the background of a 'dense forest' associated with it as well, there could be no doubt. We were looking at symbolic sexual geography! The *nymphae*, as doctors but not laymen know—and not by any means all doctors—are the small labial folds in the female genitals, seen against the 'dense forest' of pubic hair. Anyone using such technical terms as these, however, must have drawn his knowledge from books, and not popular books but anatomical textbooks or an encyclopedia, the kind of work to which young people consumed by sexual curiosity usually resort. So if my interpretation was correct, the façade of the dream concealed a defloration fantasy of a man trying to penetrate the female genitalia.[1]

I told Dora my conclusions. They must have made a forceful impression, for she immediately came up with a forgotten fragment of her dream: *that she goes calmly into her room, and reads from a large book that is lying on her desk.*[2] Here the emphasis is on the two details, she is calm, the book is large. I asked: was it like an encyclopedia? She said yes. In fact children never read forbidden material in an encyclopedia *calmly*. They are tense with alarm as they do so, looking anxiously around to see whether anyone is coming. Parents are very much in the way of such reading. However, the force of wish-fulfilment in the dream had fundamentally

[1] The defloration fantasy is the second component in this situation. Dora's emphasis on the difficulty of making progress, and the anxiety felt in her dream, point to the virginity on which she laid such stress, and that we find indicated elsewhere by the *Sistine Madonna*. These sexual ideas act as unconscious accompaniment for the wishes that were perhaps only kept secret and revolved around the suitor waiting for her in Germany. The first component of the same dream situation, as we have found, was the revenge fantasy. The two do not coincide entirely, only partially, and later we shall come upon a third and even more significant train of thought.

[2] Previously she had said 'not feeling at all sad' instead of 'calmly' (p. 80, note 4). I can cite this dream as new evidence for the accuracy of my claim in *The Interpretation of Dreams* to the effect that the first fragment of a dream to be forgotten and remembered later is always of particular importance for the understanding of that dream. In that passage I conclude that forgetting the dream also encourages its explanation by interior psychic resistance. [The first sentence of this footnote was added in 1924.]

improved the uncomfortable situation. Her father was dead, the others had gone to the cemetery. She could read what she liked in peace and quiet. Did that not mean that one of her reasons for revenge was rebellion against compulsion imposed on her by her parents? If her father was dead, she could read what she liked and love whoever she liked. At first she was unwilling to remember that she had ever read from the encyclopedia, but then she admitted that such a memory, although harmless in content, had come back to her mind. At the time when her beloved aunt was severely ill, and it had been decided that she was to go to Vienna, a *letter* came from an uncle saying that he and his family could not visit Vienna because one of his children, and thus a cousin of Dora, was dangerously ill with appendicitis. At the time she looked up the symptoms of appendicitis in the encyclopedia. From what she had read, she still recollects, she said, that characteristically there is localized pain in the body.

I now remembered that soon after her aunt's death she had suffered from what was apparently appendicitis in Vienna. I had not previously ventured to count this attack as one of the products of her hysteria. She said that she had a high temperature for the first few days, and felt the pain she had read about in the encyclopedia in her lower body. She had had cold compresses applied, but could not tolerate them. On the second day there was violent pain as she began a period; her periods had been very irregular since she fell ill. At the time she suffered almost constantly from constipation.

It was not right to regard this condition as purely hysterical. Although hysterical fever does certainly occur, it seemed high-handed to relate this odd illness of hers to hysteria rather than some organic cause affecting her at the time. I was about to give up following that trail, when she herself helped me by remembering the last addition to the dream: *she sees herself particularly clearly climbing the stairs.*

I naturally wanted a reason for that fragment. I could easily dismiss her objection to the effect that she had to go upstairs anyway, to reach the family's apartment on an upper floor, by saying that if, in her dream, she could travel from the unknown town to

Vienna and forget the railway journey, she could also ignore going up the stairs in her dream. She then went on: after the appendicitis, she said, she had had difficulty in walking because her right foot dragged. That went on for a long time, so she avoided flights of stairs where she could. Even now her foot sometimes dragged. The doctors she had consulted at her father's wish had puzzled over this very unusual legacy of appendicitis, especially as the pain in her body had not reappeared, and was nothing to do with the dragging of her foot.[1]

It was, therefore, a genuine hysterical symptom. While the fever she suffered at that time may have had an organic cause—perhaps an influenza infection without any particular localization, which is a frequent occurrence—we could be certain that the neurosis had taken over a random factor in order to use it as one of its own ways of expressing itself. So she had created an illness for herself after reading about it in the encyclopedia and being punished for that, and she had to tell herself that her punishment could not possibly be for reading that harmless article, but had come about through displacement whereby she was using it as cover to hide the reading of different, more suspect material at the same time.[2] Perhaps I might yet discover what subjects she had been reading about then.

What did the condition that aimed to imitate perityphlitis, inflammation of the tissue around the appendix, mean in Dora's case? The aftermath of her infection, the dragging of one leg which did not really follow on from perityphlitis, must conform better to the hidden and perhaps sexual significance of the clinical picture. Once explained, it could cast light on the meaning I was looking for. I tried to gain access to the puzzle. Dora's account of the dream had mentioned timings; time is not insignificant in all biological processes. So I asked when she suffered from

---

[1] A somatic connection exists between ovarian pain in the abdomen and a limp in the leg on the same side of the body as that pain, and in Dora's case it has a particularly specialized meaning, that is to say psychological superimposition and exploitation. Cf. the analogous comment in the analysis of her coughing and its connection with catarrh and loss of appetite.

[2] A typical example of the way symptoms arise from causes that apparently have nothing to do with sexuality.

appendicitis: before or after the scene by the lake? The instant answer, resolving all difficulties at one blow, was: nine months later. That meant a great deal. The alleged appendicitis had thus realized a childbirth fantasy with the few means at my patient's command, her period pains and menstrual bleeding.[1] Of course she knew the significance of that mention of nine months, and could not deny the probability that she had been reading about pregnancy and childbirth in the encyclopedia at the time. But what about her dragging leg? I could now venture on guessing. She was walking in the way you do when you stumble after missing a step, taking the wrong step. And she would indeed have taken a wrong step if she had found herself giving birth nine months after that scene by the lake. However, I had to ask something else. I am convinced that one develops such symptoms only when there is a childhood precedent for them. Memories created by later impressions do not, as I find I have to say judging by my experience so far, have the strength to express themselves as symptoms. I hardly dared to hope that she would give me the material from her childhood that I wanted, for although I would like to believe that my statement above is always true, I cannot yet really say so. Here, however, I had confirmation *at once*. Yes, she had once taken a wrong step as a child; when the family were living in B., she had slipped and missed a step going downstairs. Her foot—the same foot that she dragged later—swelled up and had to be bandaged, and she lay in bed resting it for several weeks. That happened a short time before her nervous asthma set in, in her eighth year of life.

Now I had to exploit the evidence provided by this fantasy: if you had had to give birth nine months after the scene by the lake, I suggested, and then live to this day with the consequences of taking a wrong step, it shows that in your unconscious mind you regretted the outcome of that scene. So you corrected it in your unconscious thinking. The precondition for your childbirth fantasy is that something happened before

[1] I have already indicated that most hysterical symptoms, once they have developed fully, present a fantasy of a sexual situation—that is to say, a scene of sexual intercourse, pregnancy, childbirth, lying-in, and so on.

it,[1] and that at the time you had first-hand experience of everything of which you later had to glean knowledge from the encyclopedia. You see that your love for Herr K. did not come to an end with that scene, and that, as I have claimed, it continues to this day, although unknown to you yourself. She no longer contradicted me.[2]

The work of elucidating the second dream had taken up two sessions. When, after the end of the second session, I expressed satisfaction with what had been achieved, she replied disparagingly: 'What came of all that?' I felt that she was preparing me to hear further revelations.

At our third sitting, she said, as she came in, 'Doctor, you're aware, aren't you, that this is the last time I'm coming to see you?'

[1] The defloration fantasy thus involves Herr K., and it is clear why the same part of the dream content contains material from the scene by the lake (rejection of an offer, the timespan of 2½ hours, the forest, the invitation to L.).

[2] Some additions to the meanings detected so far: The *Madonna* is clearly Dora herself, first because of the admirer who worshipped her and gave her the picture, then because she had won the love of Herr K. through her maternal affection for his children, and finally because, although a virgin, she had already had a child, in direct reference to the childbirth fantasy. Incidentally, thoughts of the Madonna are often conjured up to counter accusations that a girl has gone sexually astray, as was also the case with Dora. I had the first inkling of these connecting ideas as a doctor in a psychiatric clinic, in a case of hallucinatory confusions, which soon passed over, and were in reaction to a suspicion expressed by the patient's fiancé.

If the analysis had gone on, her maternal longing for a child would probably have revealed itself to be a hidden but strong motive for her actions.—The many questions that she had brought up recently appeared to be late descendants of the sexual curiosity that she had sought to satisfy from reading the encyclopedia. We may assume that she looked up pregnancy, childbirth, virginity, and similar subjects.—She had forgotten one of the questions that had to be fitted into the structure of the second dream situation. It could only be the question: Does Herr ——— live here? or: Where does Herr ——— live? There had to be some reason for her forgetting this apparently harmless question after asking it in the dream. I can find such a reason in her surname, which can also be used in the sense of an object,* indeed more than one, and is thus ambiguous. Unfortunately I cannot give the name in order to show how cleverly it had been used to suggest a *double entendre*. But in support of this interpretation, when we find the place where Dora's material for memories of death came from, in another part of the dream, we can also find an allusion to the name of her aunt in the sentence, 'The others have gone to the cemetery.' One would probably find an indication of another, *oral* source, one for which a dictionary does not suffice, in these ambiguous words. I would not have been surprised to hear that the source was Frau K. herself, who had slandered Dora. Dora would then generously have spared her, of all people, while pursuing the others involved with vengefulness; behind the apparently endless series of displacements thus resulting we could assume there was one simple factor, her deeply rooted homosexual love for Frau K.

I can't be aware of it when you haven't told me so.

'Well, I made up my mind to go through with it until the New Year,[1] but I'm not waiting about for a cure any longer.'

You know that you are always free to leave the analysis. But we still have work to do today. When did you come to this decision?

'Fourteen days ago, I think.'

That sounds like a maid or a governess giving two weeks' notice.

'There was a governess who did give in her notice at the K.s' house when I visited them at L. beside the lake.'

Oh? You haven't told me about her before. Please tell me now.

'She was a young girl, engaged to teach the children, and she acted very strangely towards Herr K. She never exchanged a civil word with him, didn't answer his questions or hand him anything at meals when he asked her to—in short, she treated him like thin air. In fact he wasn't much more civil to her. One or two days before the scene by the lake she took me aside, saying there was something that I ought to know. Then she told me that at a time when his wife was away for several weeks he had made advances to her, very pressing advances, asking her to be nice to him, saying there was nothing between him and his wife, and so on.'

Those are the same words he used when he was pursuing you, and when you slapped his face.

'Yes. She gave way to him, but after a short time he paid her no more attention, and since then she had hated him.'

And this governess gave notice?

'No, but she was going to. She told me that as soon as she felt Herr K. had abandoned her, she told her parents what had happened. They were good, upright people living somewhere in Germany. Her parents told her to leave the house at once, and then they wrote to say that if she didn't they wanted nothing more to do with her, and she couldn't go home again.'

Then why didn't she leave at once?

'She said she was going to wait a little to see if Herr K. changed. She couldn't bear living like that, she added, but if she didn't see any change in him then she would give notice and go away.'

---

[1] This was 31 December.

And what became of the girl?

'All I know is that she did go away.'

And there was no child as a result of this adventure?

'No.'

So now—and indeed, this generally happens—a piece of real material had emerged in the middle of the analysis and helped to solve problems that came up earlier. I felt able to tell Dora: now I know why you responded to Herr K.'s advances by slapping him in the face. It was not that you were insulted by his presumption, it was vengeful jealousy. When the governess told you her story, you made use of your ability to discard everything that didn't suit your feelings. At the moment when Herr K. said: 'There is nothing between me and my wife'—words that he had also used to the governess—he aroused new emotions in you, and the balance tipped in the other direction. You said to yourself: 'So he dares to treat me like a governess, a household servant, does he?' That injury to your pride, together with your conscious motives, were ultimately too much.[1] As evidence of the strong impression made on you by the governess's story, I suggest you think of your repeated identification with her, in the dream and in your behaviour. You tell your parents—something that we have not understood before—just as the governess wrote to her parents. Now you are dismissing me with two weeks' notice, as if I were a governess. The letter in the dream allowing you to come home is a counterpart to the governess's letter from her parents forbidding her to do so.

'Then why didn't I tell my parents at once?'

How much time did you allow to pass?

'That scene was on the last day of June; I told my mother on 14 July.'

Fourteen days again, the typical amount of notice given to a servant! I can answer your question now. You understood the poor girl very well. She didn't want to leave at once, because she still hoped or expected that Herr K.'s affection for her would revive.

[1] It may not have been irrelevant that she could have heard the same complaint about his wife, the significance of which she may well have understood, from her own father, just as I heard it in his mouth.

That must have been your motive. You waited for the period of notice to run out in order to see if he would make more advances, from which you would have concluded that he was serious, and did not mean to toy with your feelings as he did with those of the governess.

'He did send a picture-postcard a few days after he went away.'[1]

Yes, but when no more came of that, you gave your vengeful feelings free rein. I can even imagine that at the time there was still scope for part of your mind to induce him to come back to where you were staying by complaining of him.

'And he did suggest that at first,' she pointed out.—Then your longing to see him would have been satisfied—here she nodded, confirming it, which was more than I had expected—and he would have been able to give you the satisfaction that you demanded for yourself.

'What satisfaction?'

I am beginning to think that you took the approaches made by Herr K. much more seriously than you have let me know. Didn't the Ks. often discuss divorce?

'Yes, they did. At first she didn't want to divorce because of the children, and now she would like to but he doesn't want a divorce any more.'

Might you not have thought that he wanted to get divorced from his wife in order to marry you? And that now he's changed his mind about divorce because he has no substitute for her? Of course, you were very young two years ago, but you have told me yourself that your Mama was seventeen when she got engaged, and then waited two years to be married. A daughter usually follows her mother's example in love. So you wanted to wait for him, and assumed that he was just waiting for you to be of an age to become his wife.[2] I imagine that as a perfectly serious plan for

---

[1] An allusion to the engineer who was hidden behind her ego in the first dream situation.

[2] Waiting in order to achieve one's aims is to be found in the content of the first dream situation; in this fantasy of a man's waiting for his bride I can see a part of the third component of this dream, already emerging.

your life. You can't even tell me that any such intention on Herr K.'s part could be ruled out; you have already told me enough that points directly to such an intention.[1] Nor is it refuted by his behaviour in L. You didn't let him finish what he was saying, so you do not know what he wanted to tell you. And incidentally, the plan would not by any means have been impracticable. Your Papa's relationship with Frau K., which you probably encouraged so long only for that very reason, offered you an assurance that she could have been induced to agree to divorce, and you can always get your way with your Papa. In fact, if the temptation you felt in L. had not ended as it did, that would have been the only possible solution for all concerned. I also think that is why you so much regretted the way it did end, adjusting it to suit you in a fantasy that appeared as appendicitis. It must have been a great disappointment when you found out that the result of your complaining of Herr K. was not a renewal of his advances to you, but denial of what you said and invective against you on his part. You admit that nothing infuriates you as much as being suspected of having imagined the scene beside the lake. I know now what you don't want to be reminded of: it is that you imagined he was making advances to you in earnest, and would not desist until you married him.

She had been listening without, as usual, raising objections. She seemed to be moved, said goodbye in the most charming way, wishing me every happiness in the New Year, left—and did not come back. Her father, who came to see me several times after that, assured me that she would change her mind; you could see, he told me, how much she longed for the treatment to go on. But he was probably not being entirely honest. He had supported the course of treatment while he could still hope that I would 'disabuse' Dora of the notion that his relationship with Frau K. was anything other than friendship. His interest lapsed when he saw that I had no intention of doing that. I knew she would not be back. It was an undisputed act of revenge for her to break off the

---

[1] In particular a remark that he had made when sending her the Christmas present of a writing-case when they were still all together in B.

treatment so suddenly, when I had every expectation of bringing the analysis to a happy conclusion, thus dashing all those hopes. It also accounted for her tendency to self-harming. A doctor like me, who wakes the worst demons that dwell imperfectly controlled in the human breast in order to fight them, must expect that he will not always get off unscathed himself. Could I have induced the girl to go on with her treatment if I had found a role for myself in our relationship, exaggerating the value to me of her continuing, and showing a warm interest in her, although— qualified by my position as a doctor—it would have been only a substitute for the affection that she longed for? I do not know. As some of the factors putting up resistance remain unknown in any case, I have always avoided such playacting, contenting myself with the less demanding skill of a psychologist. For all my theoretical interest, and my medical efforts to help, I tell myself that bounds must necessarily be set to the influence I can bring to bear on a mind, and I respect the patient's own will and insight.

Nor do I know whether Herr K. would have been more successful if he had been told that Dora's slap by no means meant a final 'No', but reflected the jealousy recently aroused in her, while her strongest emotions still worked in his favour. If he had ignored that first 'No' and continued to make advances with convincing passion, he could easily have succeeded in gaining the girl's affections in spite of all difficulties. But I think she might just as easily have merely been provoked into expressing her vengeful wishes at yet greater length. We can never calculate the side on which the decision will come down when there are conflicting motives: will the repression be removed or intensified? An inability to meet the *real* demands of love is one of the essential characteristics of neurosis; the patients are dominated by the opposition of reality and fantasy. They will flee from what they long for most intensely in their fantasies if they encounter it in real life, and they are most likely to abandon themselves to fantasies when they no longer need to fear their realization. The barriers erected by repression can fall to an assault by violent emotions with real causes, a neurosis may yet be overcome by reality. However, in general we cannot work out in whom and by what means such a cure may take place.[1]

---

[1] A few more comments follow on the structure of Dora's dream, which cannot be well enough understood for me to try to create a synthesis. The fantasy of revenge on her father is part of a façade: she has left home of her own accord, her father falls ill and then dies . . . She then goes home, the others are already at the cemetery. She goes up to her room, not feeling at all sad, and calmly reads the encyclopedia. We also have two allusions to her other act of revenge, the one she put into practice, by letting her parents find a farewell letter: the letter (in her dream of Mama) and mention of the funeral ceremony for the aunt who was her model.—This fantasy veils over ideas of revenge on Herr K., and she found a way of expressing them in her behaviour to me. The maidservant—the invitation—the forest—the period of 2½ hours all come from the material of the events in L. Her memory of the governess, and her correspondence with her parents, are linked to the letter in the dream content giving her permission to go home. Her rejection of company, her decision to go alone, can be translated thus: Because you have treated me like a servant, I will turn away from you, go my own way and never marry.—In other places material from fantasies of her unconsciously continuing love for Herr K. shows through these idea of revenge: I would have waited to become your wife—the defloration—childbirth. Finally, it is in the part of her fourth and most deeply hidden circle of ideas, that of her love for Frau K., that the defloration fantasy is seen from the man's point of view (identification with her admirer who is now far away) and that in two places there are clear allusions to ambiguous language (does Herr —— live here?) and to the non-oral source of her sexual knowledge, the encyclopedia. Cruel and sadistic feelings are expressed in this dream.

IV

AFTERWORD

WHILE I have called this record the fragment of an analysis, the reader will have discovered that it is incomplete to a much wider extent than might be expected from that title. It is only right for me to try to explain the reasons for omissions that were far from being a matter of chance.

I have left out a series of conclusions from the analysis because, for one thing, when it was cut short I was not sure enough of them, and for another, it needed to be continued until we reached an overall result. On other occasions, where I felt it was permissible I have indicated the probable conclusions to which some solutions would have led. I have entirely omitted any account of the technique—not something to be taken for granted, but it is the only way of extracting, from the raw material of the patient's ideas, its content of valuable unconscious thoughts. The disadvantage of leaving out such an account is that the reader cannot confirm that the way I presented this process was correct. However, I found it entirely impracticable to deal with the technique of an analysis and the internal structure of a case of hysteria at the same time; it would have been almost impossible for me, and would probably not have been a pleasant experience for the reader. The technique requires separate presentation, clarified by examples taken from many very different cases, and can be seen without reference to the particular case concerned. Nor have I tried to give reasons here for the psychological assumptions that, as I describe it, cast light on psychic phenomena. A superficial account of the process would achieve nothing; a thorough one would be a major work in itself. I can only assure my readers that, without owing allegiance to any one psychological system, I have studied those phenomena that are revealed by the observation of psychoneurotics, and that I had then adjusted my ideas until they seemed to me to do justice to the connections between what I had observed. I am not proud to have steered clear of speculation;

however, material for my hypotheses has been gained by the closest and most extensive observation. My firm stance in the matter
of the unconscious mind was likely to arouse particular hostility,
in that I work with unconscious ideas, trains of thought, and
emotions as if they were as obviously suitable subjects for psychological study as all conscious ideas, but I am sure that anyone
embarking on the study of the same phenomena by that method
will inevitably come round to my point of view in spite of any
admonitions from philosophers.

The same professional colleagues who consider my theory of
hysteria to be purely psychological, and have therefore dismissed it
from the first as unable to explain a pathological problem, will see
from this account that their objection unjustly ascribes a characteristic of the technique to the theory itself. It is only the therapeutic
technique that is purely psychological; the theory by no means
neglects to indicate the organic basis of a neurosis, although it does
not seek it in pathological and anatomical change, and replaces the
chemical changes to be expected as a result, as something not yet
fully understood, by the temporary nature of an organic function.
I suppose no one will deny that there is an organic factor in the
sexual function, which I see as the basis for hysteria and for psychoneuroses in general. A theory of sexual life will not, I assume, be
able to dismiss the idea that certain sexual matters provoke arousal.
The effects of intoxication and abstention in the chronic use of certain toxic substances are closest to genuine psychoneuroses of all
the clinical pictures that we learn about during clinical training.

In this account, however, I have left out what we can say today
about 'somatic compliance', the roots of perversion in infancy, the
erogenous zones, and the tendency to bisexuality; I have only
indicated the passages in which the analysis touches on these
organic foundations of the symptoms. No more than that could be
done from an isolated case, and I had the same reasons as I gave
above to avoid a mere fleeting mention of those factors. What
I have said here gives plenty of scope for further work based on a
large number of analyses.

However, I hoped to achieve two aims in publishing this
account, even though it is not complete. First, to offer a complement

to my book on *The Interpretation of Dreams*, showing how that otherwise useless skill can be employed in revealing what is hidden and repressed in the life of the mind. In analysing the two dreams described here, I took into consideration the technique of dream-interpretation, which is similar to psychoanalytic technique. Secondly, I wanted to arouse interest in a series of relationships which are still entirely unknown to science today, because they can be discovered only by the use of that particular procedure. It is likely that no one has been able to form a real idea of the complexity of the psychic processes involved in hysteria, the juxtaposition of very different kinds of emotions, the link between opposites, repressions and displacements, and much else. Janet's* emphasis on the *idée fixe* that transforms itself into a symptom is nothing but a very deficient reduction of these phenomena to a set scheme. Nor can we help but assume that cases of arousal of which the conscious mind lacks any appropriate idea react on each other differently, run a different course, and lead to forms of expression different from those that we call 'normal', the content of which is clear to the conscious mind. Once that has been clarified, there is nothing to prevent our understanding of a therapy that neutralizes neurotic symptoms by turning ideas of the first kind into normal ideas.

I was also anxious to show that sexuality does not just play the part of a *deus ex machina* appearing once, and once only, to intervene somewhere in the way the processes characteristic of hysteria work, but is the driving force of every individual symptom and every individual expression of a symptom. The manifestations of the disorder, I may say straight out, are *the patient's sexual activity*. A single case will never be able to prove that such a principle is a general one, but I can only go on repeating, because I never find anything to the contrary, that sexuality is the key to the problem of psychoneuroses and indeed neuroses in general. Those who reject that idea will never be able to solve it. I have yet to see any investigations disproving or qualifying my hypothesis. All the objections to it I have encountered so far were expressions of personal distaste or disbelief, and it is enough to counter them with Charcot's remark: 'Ça n'empêche pas d'exister.'*

Nor is the case from which I have taken a fragment of its clinical history and treatment, publishing it here, suitable to cast the right light on the value of psychoanalytical therapy. Not just the brevity of the treatment, which lasted barely three months, but another factor germane to the case prevented the treatment from leading, as usual, to an improvement obvious to the patient and the patient's family, and more or less equivalent to a complete cure. Such a happy outcome is achieved where the symptoms of the disorder have depended entirely on the internal conflict between feelings about sexuality. In such cases the health of patients improves to an extent determined by the doctor's success in contributing to the solution of their psychic problems by translating pathogenical into normal material. The course of events is different where symptoms have been put to the service of other motives in a patient's life, as Dora's had been for the last two years. We are surprised, and could easily be led astray, to discover that the patient's condition has not noticeably changed even when the work of analysis is far advanced. In reality, however, this is not so deplorable; the patient's symptoms may disappear not during analysis but some time later, when the relationship to the doctor is not so close. A postponement of the cure or improvement is really caused only by the person of the doctor.

I must range a little farther afield to explain this fact. During psychoanalytic treatment, we may say that the development of new symptoms is regularly in abeyance. However, the neurosis has not gone away, but is actively forming a special kind of usually unconscious ideas, which we may call *transferences*.

What are transferences? They are new editions, imitations of feelings and fantasies, that are to be aroused and brought into the conscious mind as the analysis proceeds, characteristically by substituting the person of the doctor for someone who was previously part of the patient's life. To put it another way: a whole series of earlier psychic experiences are revived, not as memories of the past but as a relationship to the doctor in the present. There are instances of transference that differed in content from their model in nothing but the substitution. They are thus—to stay with the same metaphor—simple reprints, new, unchanged editions of

the same story. Others are more elaborately devised; they have
undergone moderation of their content, *sublimation*, as I term it,
and can even move into the conscious mind by evoking some cleverly assessed real feature of the doctor's personality or circumstances. These are revised editions, not just reprints.

If you begin studying the theory of analytical technique, you
soon come to see that transference is a necessary and requisite part
of it. In practice at least, you will convince yourself that there is no
avoiding it by any means whatever, and that this last symptom
created by the disorder has to be fought like all the others. And
this part of the work is by far the most difficult. Interpreting
dreams, extracting unconscious feelings and memories from the
ideas expressed by the patient, and similar translation skills are
easily learnt: the text is almost always supplied by the patient. But
the therapist has to detect transference almost on his own from
slight indications, and without being high-handed. However, it
must be done, since it will be used to establish the nature of all the
obstacles making the material inaccessible to treatment, and since
a sense of conviction that the therapist is right about the structural
connections in the patient's mind will come only when the transference has been resolved.

It may be considered a grave disadvantage of what is in any case
an uncomfortable procedure that it gives the doctor more work,
by creating a new genre of pathological products, and that the
existence of transferences in analytical treatment may even harm
the patient. Both ideas would be wrong. The doctor's workload is
not increased by transference; it is a matter of indifference to him
whether he has to overcome a feeling aroused in the patient in
connection with his own person or with someone else. And successful treatment involving transference does not force patients to
do any more than they would have done for themselves anyway. If
patients can also recover from neurosis in clinics where psychoanalytical treatment is excluded, and it could be claimed that hysteria is cured not by the method but by the doctor, if patients
develop a kind of blind dependence on the doctor and long-term
attachment to him for ridding them of their symptoms by hyp-
notic suggestion, the scientific explanation for all this is to be seen

in the 'transferences' felt by patients transferring their feelings to that doctor. A psychoanalytical cure does not create the transference, it merely reveals it, like other matters hidden in the life of a patient's mind. The only difference is that patients spontaneously develop exclusively affectionate and friendly transferences to effect their cure; where that cannot happen, they break off treatment as quickly as possible, uninfluenced by a doctor whom they do not consider likeable. In psychoanalysis, on the other hand, in line with a different set of motives, all emotions, including hostility, are aroused, once in the conscious mind they can be exploited for the analysis, and in the process the transference is repeatedly dissolved. Transference, destined to be the greatest obstacle to psychoanalysis, becomes its most powerful therapeutic aid if the therapist always succeeds in detecting its nature and translating it for the patient.[1]

I had to say a few words about transference, because that factor is the only way in which I can cast light on the particular aspects of Dora's analysis. Its advantage, which makes it suitable for a first, introductory publication on my subject, and its particular transparency are closely connected with its great disadvantage, which led to the treatment's premature conclusion. I did not succeed in mastering the transference in time; the readiness which made my patient willing to place part of the pathogenic material at my disposal made me forget to look carefully for the first signs of transference, which she was preparing to make using another part of the same material still unknown to me. At first it was clear that in fantasy I replaced her father, which seemed obvious in view of the age-difference between us. She also kept consciously comparing me with him, anxiously trying to find out whether I was being perfectly honest with her, because her father 'always preferred secrecy and going the long way round'. Then, when she had her first dream, in which she warned herself to leave treatment just as she had left Herr K.'s house on that past occasion, I ought to have been warned myself. I should have told her: 'Now you have transferred your feelings for Herr K. to me. Have you seen anything to

---

[1] (Added in 1923.) What I have said here about transference is continued in the technical essay on 'transference love' ['Observations on Transference-Love', SE xii. 157–71].

make you conclude that I have bad intentions similar to Herr K.'s (directly or in some form of sublimation), have you noticed anything about me or heard anything of me that compels you to feel the same kind of affection as you did for Herr K?' Then her attention would have been drawn to some detail of our acquaintanceship, something about my person or my circumstances, behind which something analogous but incomparably more important regarding Herr K. was concealed, and when I had resolved that transference the analysis would have had access to fresh, and probably genuine, material from her memory. However, I had failed to hear that first warning; I thought there was plenty of time, since she had not yet reached other stages of transference, and she was still providing material for analysis. The transference thus took me by surprise, and because of something unknown to me, call it X, in which I reminded her of Herr K., she was avenging herself on me as she wanted to avenge herself on Herr K., and leaving me because she thought that he had deceived and abandoned her. She was *acting out* a large part of her memories and fantasies instead of reproducing them during treatment. Of course I could not know what X was: I assume it was something to do with money, or alternatively was jealousy of another woman patient who had kept in touch with my family after she was cured. When transference appears early in analysis, it takes an obscure and slow course, but its survival is better secured from sudden, irresistible opposition.

The transference is represented by several clear allusions in Dora's second dream. One was when she told me, as I did not yet know but learned two days later, that we had only *two hours* of work ahead of us, referring to the time that she had spent in front of the picture of the *Sistine Madonna*, and that by dint of correcting herself (from two hours instead of two-and-a-half hours) she said that was the time it would take to go the rest of the way round the lake. Then there was the waiting and her difficult progress in the dream, which related to the young man in Germany and arose from her idea of waiting until Herr K. could marry her; she had already expressed that in the transference a few days earlier. The treatment, she said, was taking too long for her liking; she would never have the patience to wait so long. During the first weeks she had shown enough insight to accept, without any such objection, my telling her that it would take about a year to cure her entirely. And then there was her rejection of a companion in her dream: she would rather go alone. That also derived from her visit to the Dresden Gallery, and I was not to hear about this until the day appointed for telling me. She probably had in mind something like: As all men are so horrible I would rather not marry at all, and this is my revenge.[1]

Where feelings of cruelty and motives for revenge that have been exploited in real life to maintain symptoms are transferred to the doctor during treatment, before he has had time to dissociate them from himself by tracing them back to their sources, it is not surprising that the condition of his patient does not respond to his therapeutic endeavours. How could the patient be more effectively revenged than by demonstrating the doctor's helplessness and lack of ability in her own person? All the same, I am inclined to think that there is considerable therapeutic value even in such a fragmentary treatment as Dora's.

I had no news of my patient's state of health and thus of the outcome of her treatment until a year and a quarter after she had ended it, and I had written this record. On a day that is not without ulterior significance, on the first of April—and we know how significant times were to Dora—she came to see me to end her

---

[1] The further I move in time from the end of this analysis, the more likely it seems to me that my technical mistake was as follows: I failed to guess in good time that her homosexual (gynaecophile) love for Frau K. was the strongest unconscious current in the life of her mind, and to tell her so. I ought to have worked out that no one but Frau K. could be the main source of her knowledge of sexual matters—the same person by whom she had then been blamed for her interest in them. It was very striking that she knew all about improper subjects, and would never face the question of how she knew these things. I ought to have looked harder at that puzzle in search of the motive for such a strange repression. The second dream would then have told me. The unthinking desire for revenge expressed by that dream was particularly suitable for covering up the current running the other way, the magnanimity with which she forgave her beloved friend's treachery and hid from everyone the fact that Frau K. herself had given her knowledge of things for which she was to be suspected of immorality later. Before I had recognized the importance of the homosexual current in psychoneurotics, I often came to a dead end or found myself utterly bewildered in the treatment of such cases.

story and ask for help again. However, a glance at her expression told me that she did not mean her request seriously. She told me that for four or five weeks after she had left treatment she had been, as she put it, in 'great confusion'. But then there was a great improvement, her attacks of illness came less often, and her spirits lifted. In May of the year that had just passed one of Herr and Frau K.'s children, who had always been sickly, died. She took this sad event as the occasion to visit the Ks. and express her condolences, and they welcomed her as if nothing had happened. She was reconciled to them, as her own way of taking her revenge and bringing the whole story to what, for her, was a satisfactory conclusion. She told Frau K.: I know you are having an affair with Papa. Frau K. did not deny it. She made Herr K. admit that the scene by the lake, which he had disputed, had been as she said, and took her Papa that news, which vindicated her. She had not been in touch with the family again.

She was then very well until mid-October, when she lost her voice again, and did not get it back for six weeks. Surprised to hear that, I ask if there was any reason for it, and I heard that the attack was linked to a severe shock suffered when she saw someone being run over by a vehicle in the street. At last she told me that the victim of the accident had been none other than Herr K. She met him in the street one day; he was coming towards her at a spot where there was a great deal of traffic, stopped in front of her as if confused, and as if he had lost thought of all else he let himself be knocked down.[1] She was able to assure herself that he had escaped without serious injury. Something in her still reacted when she heard about Papa's relationship with Frau K., she said, but she was not involved with that any more. She told me that she lived for her studies and had no intention of marrying.

She was asking my help for neuralgia by both day and night on the right-hand side of her face. How long, I asked, had she had it? 'For exactly fourteen days.'[2]—I could not help smiling, since

---

[1] An interesting addition to the cases of indirect suicide attempts in my *Psychopathology of Everyday Life.*

[2] See the significance of this length of time and its connection to the subject of revenge in the analysis of her second dream.

I could prove to her that she had read a newspaper story about me in the paper exactly fourteen days ago, as she agreed (this was in 1902).

The apparent neuralgia, then, corresponded to punishment of herself, regret for having slapped Herr K.'s face beside the lake, and the transference of her vengeful feelings to me. I do not know just what kind of help she wanted to ask me for, but I promised to forgive her for denying me the satisfaction of liberating her far more entirely from her disorder.

It is years now since that last visit of hers. Since then, the girl herself has been married, to the same young man, unless I am much mistaken, who was mentioned at the beginning of my analysis of her second dream. Just as the first dream described her turning against the man she loved and back to her father, taking refuge from life in illness, that second dream showed that she would break away from her father and return to real life.

EXPLANATORY NOTES

4 *roman à clef*: a novel based on real events, where a key (*clef*) to the characters would reveal the identities of the actual people involved.

12 *Not art . . . be shown!*: from the scene 'A Witch's Kitchen' in *Faust, Part One* (1808) by Johann Wolfgang Goethe (1749–1832).

13 *tabes*: degeneration of nerves in the spinal cord, usually the result of syphilis, and leading to pains, paralysis, and loss of coordination and proprioception (awareness of one's own body), among other symptoms.

15 *taboparesis*: a form of syphilis including symptoms of tabes dorsalis.

17 *dyspnoea*: difficulty in breathing.

20 *fluor albus*: a whitish vaginal discharge.

   Mantegazza's Physiology of Love: Paolo Mantegazza (1831–1910), Italian neurologist whose many works included popular accounts of physiology and sexuality.

25 *inter urinas et faeces nascimur*: 'we are born between urine and faeces'. Freud ascribes this saying to an unnamed Church Father. It has not proved possible to locate it in patristic sources, and it may well be apocryphal. It does, however, appear, ascribed only to a 'Church Father', in the tenth edition (1867) of a well-known textbook of anatomy by Josef Hyrtl, who was then teaching in Vienna. I am very grateful to Johannes Zachhuber for this information.

31 *Semmering*: a mountain resort with many hotels, some 70 miles south of Vienna.

33 *Charcot clinic*: Jean-Marie Charcot (1825–93), French neurologist; in 1882 he established a neurological clinic at the Salpêtrière hospital in Paris, where Freud studied in 1885–6.

36 *Paracelsus*: a play (1897) by Arthur Schnitzler (1864–1931), in which the sixteenth-century healer Theophrastus Bombastus von Hohenheim, known as Paracelsus (1493–1541), revisits an old friend, Cyprian, in Basel. Cyprian's wife Justina was formerly in love with Paracelsus. By hypnotizing her, Paracelsus first reawakes and then dissolves her former affection for him, thus leaving the marriage more secure. Paracelsus, contrasted here with orthodox medicine, could easily seem to Freud to prefigure psychoanalysis.

40 *per os*: Latin: 'by mouth'.

41 *J'appelle un chat un chat*: literally 'I call a cat a cat', i.e. I call a spade a spade.

42 *Psychopathia sexualis*: a study of sexual abnormality (1896) by the German psychiatrist Richard von Krafft-Ebing (1840–1902), who in 1873 moved

to Austria, where he first directed a clinic and then taught as professor of psychiatry in Graz until his death.

45 *Gospels . . . new wine into old bottles*: Matt. 9: 17; Mark 2: 22; Luke 5: 37.

Wernicke's: Carl Wernicke (1848–1905), German psychiatrist; Freud is probably referring to his *Grundriss der Psychiatrie* (*Outline of Psychiatry*, 1900).

47 *Oedipus*: mythical king of Thebes in Greece, and subject of Sophocles' tragedy *King Oedipus*. Because of a prophecy that if he grew up he would kill his father, the child Oedipus was exposed on a mountainside at birth (the Greek way of disposing of unwanted children), but he was saved and reared by shepherds. As an adult, he met and killed his real father Laius, king of Thebes, not knowing his identity, and married Laius' widow Jocasta, thus unwittingly committing parricide and incest. This myth provided Freud with the label 'Oedipus complex' for a male child's supposed antagonism for his father and desire for his mother.

49 *Calmly . . . see you go*: from the ballad 'Ritter Toggenburg' (1798) by Friedrich Schiller (1759–1805). The lines are spoken by the lady who is unable to return the knight of Toggenburg's love. Deeply grieved, he goes crusading in the Holy Land and returns to find that the lady has just taken the veil; in his loyalty, he spends the rest of his life as a hermit underneath her window. The first line quoted could mean, out of context, 'I may appear calm to you', and Freud seems to have misunderstood it in this way.

51 *Medea*: the figure from Greek mythology who appears in Euripides' tragedy *Medea* and many later plays. A princess in the remote country of Colchis, she used her magical powers to help the Greek hero Jason to steal the Golden Fleece kept there, but on returning with him to Greece she found him more attracted by Creusa, daughter of King Creon of Corinth; in anger, Medea killed not only Creusa but also her and Jason's two children. For a discussion of Freud's use of the story, see the Introduction, p. xli.

52 *without quarrelling*: Freud has here smuggled in a quotation from Schiller's tragedy *Wallensteins Tod* (*The Death of Wallenstein*, 1799), II. ii: 'The world is narrow, wide the mind of man. | Our thoughts make easy neighbours for each other, | But roughly jostling, things crowd close in space' (Friedrich Schiller, *The Robbers; Wallenstein*, tr. F. J. Lamport (Harmondsworth: Penguin, 1979), 350).

53 *gynaecophile*: literally 'woman-loving'.

56 *I suddenly woke up to find Herr K. standing before me*: the reader familiar with classic German literature, as Freud was, will hear ghostly echoes of two famous fictional scenes which may have helped to shape Freud's account. In Schiller's *Wallensteins Tod*, Wallenstein recounts a dream of being knocked unconscious on the battlefield, from which he awoke to find Octavio Piccolomini standing before him (line 934); he does not

know that Octavio is to bring about his death. In the story *Die Marquise von O . . .* (1808) by Heinrich von Kleist (1778–1811), the Marquise recalls waking from sleep on a sofa and seeing a servant stealing away, whom she suspects of having impregnated her while she slept. See Schiller, *The Robbers; Wallenstein*, tr. Lamport, 355; Heinrich von Kleist, *The Marquise of O—and Other Stories*, tr. David Luke and Nigel Reeves (Harmondsworth: Penguin, 1978), 103.

64 *Franzensbad*: a resort, then in the Austrian province of Bohemia, now Františkovy Lázně in the Czech Republic.

66 *box*: after using the German word *Dose*, Freud here inserts the English word 'box' and its Greek equivalent. This seems connected with a passage in *The Interpretation of Dreams* about different German words for 'box' and the link between the English word 'box' and the German *Büchse*, literally 'tin can' but also 'a vulgar term for the female genitals' (*The Interpretation of Dreams*, tr. Joyce Crick, Oxford World's Classics (Oxford: Oxford University Press, 1999), 121). Here, Freud is providing evidence for the sexual meaning that the lady unconsciously attributes to her box.

Venus: the classical goddess of love, represented as born from the waves and coming to land in a hollow shell, most famously in Botticelli's *Birth of Venus*.

67 *W. Fliess*: for Freud's relationship with Wilhelm Fliess see the Introduction, p. xxxix.

89 *an object*: the name Bauer, besides its obvious meaning 'farmer', can also mean 'a pawn at chess' or 'a bird-cage'. Freud's *double entendre* may allude to the vulgar expression 'den kalten Bauer aufwärmen', i.e. to practise fellatio. The allusion to the name of Dora's aunt, Malvine Bauer, is, however, mysterious.

98 *Janet's*: Pierre Janet (1859–1947), French psychologist and psychotherapist, who worked especially on hysteria.

'Ça n'empêche pas d'exister': 'That doesn't prevent them from existing.'

The Oxford World's Classics Website

www.worldsclassics.co.uk

- Browse the full range of Oxford World's Classics online

- Sign up for our monthly e-alert to receive information on new titles

- Read extracts from the Introductions

- Listen to our editors and translators talk about the world's greatest literature with our Oxford World's Classics audio guides

- Join the conversation, follow us on Twitter at OWC_Oxford

- Teachers and lecturers can order inspection copies quickly and simply via our website

www.worldsclassics.co.uk